Bringing CBT Supervision to Life

Bringing CBT Supervision to Life provides supervisors of Cognitive Behavioural Therapy (CBT) with an invaluable resource for reflecting on their current supervisory style and methods and developing their repertoire of skills in this area.

Research suggests that routine supervision practices over-rely on verbal case discussion, and this can limit opportunities for more active and experiential methods such as role-play, chair work or self-practice of CBT methods that deepen therapist understanding of theory and practice. This book explains why supervision needs to be a more active experience as well as how to do this. It provides readers with specific chapters dedicated to different experiential methods and explains the rationale and benefits of utilising each. Case studies are used throughout to help illustrate the challenges for CBT supervisors, and each chapter contains handouts and worksheets to use with supervisees. The author draws upon their experience of researching supervision and providing extensive supervision and supervisor training to create a resource that supervisors of any level of expertise can dip into when looking to freshen up their skills.

The book is primarily aimed at practitioners who provide supervision or supervision of supervision for CBT therapists and trainees. It will be an accessible resource for both new and experienced supervisors in healthcare, education and private practice.

Jason Roscoe is a BABCP-accredited cognitive behavioural therapist and supervisor. He is an experienced trainer of supervisors and has published research on supervision practices within CBT. He has a particular interest in supervisory drift and the interpersonal processes within supervision and regularly presents at conferences nationally and internationally on these topics.

‘This very readable and accessible book offers both the new and experienced CBT clinical supervisor a wonderfully layered approach to addressing the many contemporary issues encountered in supervisory practice. It will make a real difference in how a supervisor makes sense of the many moving parts of CBT clinical supervision.’

John Storey, *CBT Pathway Lead for PG Cert Supervision Skills, Psychological Therapies Training Centre, Greater Manchester Mental Health Foundation Trust*

‘Whether you’re a seasoned supervisor or just beginning your journey, this book provides practical guidance, and a compassionate lens through which to view the complexities of supporting others in their professional development. It is thoughtfully written and deeply grounded in both theory and real-world practice, offering a rich, reflective exploration of the supervisory relationship. A must-read for those committed to fostering growth, resilience, and excellence in clinical practice’.

Sarah Priestley, *programme lead for the CBT Training Programme at the University of Lincoln*

‘Informed by the current evidence-based literature on supervision, this practical, easy-to-read guide to becoming a more effective CBT supervisor explores the barriers to delivering good supervisory practice in an honest, balanced and relatable way. Using case examples to illustrate and address the common pitfalls experienced across different service settings, this book is a must-read for all those (CBT supervisors) who want to improve their supervision skills.’

Dr Madeleine Tatham, *clinical psychologist and lecturer on the PG CBT for Eating Disorders Programme, University of Sheffield*

‘This book provides us with the answers to the core questions of what makes an effective supervisor and gives us plenty of food for thought surrounding how we might continue to develop. We’re given accessible and useful tips, that will be of significant help to both newly qualified and highly experienced individuals. Heartily recommended reading for anyone looking to step beyond the basics of clinical supervision.’

Alex Preston, *clinical lead for the Staffordshire University High-Intensity CBT Course*

Bringing CBT Supervision to Life

Using Active Methods to Enhance Therapist Skills

Jason Roscoe

Routledge
Taylor & Francis Group
LONDON AND NEW YORK

First published 2027
by Routledge
4 Park Square, Milton Park, Abingdon, Oxon OX14 4RN

and by Routledge
605 Third Avenue, New York, NY 10158

Routledge is an imprint of the Taylor & Francis Group, an informa business

British Library Cataloguing-in-Publication Data
A catalogue record for this book is available from the British Library

ISBN: 978-1-032-96762-2 (hbk)
ISBN: 978-1-032-96761-5 (pbk)
ISBN: 978-1-003-59062-0 (ebk)

DOI: 10.4324/9781003590620

Typeset in Times New Roman
by Apex CoVantage, LLC

Contents

Acknowledgements

There are a whole host of individuals and organisations who in their own way have supported the development of the ideas that are contained within this book. First, to the BABCP for supporting my work through a series of skills classes and conference presentations. A special thanks is given to the members of the BABCP Supervision SIG for their support and encouragement over the years. There are other organisations who have been instrumental in spreading the word about active methods in CBT supervision including EABCT, Rod and Shirley at CBT Reach, University of Bath, the University of Sheffield, the University of Exeter and Greater Manchester Mental Health NHS Foundation Trust. There have been certain individuals who have been key to informing and supporting my ideas over a number of years, so a huge thanks go to the likes of Mathew Pugh, Tobyn Bell, John Storey, Mark Latham and Pete Moseley. Finally, a special thanks to Grace at Routledge for backing the idea of this book and to all of the supervisors and supervisees that have contributed to various research projects that I have undertaken.

Foreword

When I started providing CBT supervision 30 odd years ago, the modus operandum was case discussion. The supervisor would ask questions and make suggestions which were (sometimes) gratefully received by the supervisees. If the supervisees were trainees, audio or video might be played as part of the course requirements. The occasional bit of role-play might also be used if both parties were feeling adventurous. But the predominant method remained case discussion. Whilst this focus enabled learning to occur, and was undoubtedly better than no supervision at all, it did not fit very well with the literature on maximising learning. Unfortunately, judging from workshops I have run since, this situation seems not to have changed much in the intervening years.

Choice of the more active methods depends on the main need that is evident in the supervision issue brought by supervisees. The normative function of supervision can be met through 'live' supervision by viewing audio/video clips of supervisees' clinical sessions, or by asking them to practice a particular skill. Both these methods enable the supervisor to assess supervisees' proficiency and give them feedback accordingly. The formative function is often addressed initially by the supervisor modelling an approach, followed by supervisees then practising it themselves and gaining feedback. Restorative needs frequently entail greater emotional involvement from supervisees. Suitable methods here might include role-play to develop greater understanding and empathy for the patient, chair work to help supervisees engage with their different parts, or Self-Practice/Self-Reflection (SP/SR) to apply the CBT model to themselves.

Active supervision methods can be exciting, engaging, moving, challenging, transformative and fun. The theoretical rationale for their effectiveness is compelling. So, why on earth are they so underused?

There are several reasons why case discussion is usually favoured. Firstly, it is familiar and often the cultural norm. Secondly, supervisees may respond favourably to its use, thus reinforcing the supervisor's behaviour. Additionally, there may be beliefs held by both parties that it is effective. And finally, emotionally it is comfortable. Probably too comfortable.

Supervisors are sometimes unfamiliar with certain active methods. Also, the supervisor may be reluctant to use methods that might make supervisees uncomfortable.

There may be beliefs that such methods are unnecessary. Many of them can evoke anxiety in supervisees and, sometimes, supervisor. Additionally, they can be more time-consuming, though this is not necessarily so.

Given these 'pulls' towards case discussion and 'pushes' away from active methods, what can convince us to use the latter more often?

This book certainly can. It fills a gap in the market because of its unique features. Unlike other books on CBT supervision, it has an entire chapter devoted to each specific active method. It provides a strong rationale for the use of each method, examines potential barriers to its use, especially supervisor/supervisee beliefs, and gives practical guidance on how to implement it, including exercises for the reader to complete.

Part I has an appropriate emphasis on therapist skill development. Whilst the need for such skill development may be fairly evident during training when there is an intense period of learning, it is also needed beyond training. Even very experienced therapists are not immune to 'drift'; indeed, they may actually be more prone to it. The rationale for getting more active in supervision is made comprehensively in this section.

Part II deals with the practicalities of how to start off on the right foot. Establishing mutual expectations, addressing reservations, and having a frank and open discussion about active methods are all key elements of contracting in supervision and are crucial. In other words, the process of contracting is far more important than the outcome (the contract itself).

The third and final section of this book considers each active method in turn. What is particularly helpful here is how attention is drawn to the importance of a good supervision question. Through careful probing from the supervisor, the initial question brought by the supervisee can be narrowed down to a more specific focus about formulation, treatment technique, or the therapeutic alliance. This will then usually invite the use of specific active methods that enable deeper learning to occur. Live methods such as SP/SR, Deliberate Practice and Chair work are all discussed in detail in Part III of the book, including how one active method can often naturally lead on to another in the same supervision session.

I thoroughly recommend this important book to you. Its main message needs to be shouted from the rooftops. I urge you to implement the ideas in your supervisory practice. Maybe start from the radical position of only using case discussion as a last resort. In the words of author Paulo Cuelo, 'Be brave. Take risks. Nothing can substitute experience'.

Mark Latham
Cognitive Behavioural Therapist and Supervisor
Former Head of Training at Newcastle CBT Centre

Figures

Tables

Chapter 1

Introduction

It is almost 30 years since Liese and Beck (1997) stated that 'Cognitive therapy supervision can be as complex and challenging as cognitive therapy itself. Thus it is surprising that so little has been written about cognitive therapy supervision' (p. 114). CBT supervision remains a complex and challenging undertaking, perhaps more so given the expansion of CBT from a short-term therapy aimed at treating anxiety disorders and depression to one where protocols have been developed and tested for severe and enduring problems such as eating disorders and personality disorders (e.g. Davidson, 2008; Fairburn, 2008).

The increasing demands on CBT supervisors because of the sheer breadth of modern CBT is summarised by Corrie and Lane (2016):

> Supervisors today need to ensure that they are well-versed in the theoretical and technical requirements of a range of disorder specific treatment protocols, know how to guide their supervisees in constructing individually tailored intervention plans for diverse and atypical clinical presentations and remain informed about emerging theories, models, techniques and research in what is a rapidly expanding field.
>
> (p2)

All of these factors must be held in mind whilst also trying to make the supervisee feel as safe as possible in what can be a threatening environment (Ellis et al., 2014). From the anxiety of feeling deskilled in a new role, through to the shame that can arise when showing videos of one's work to peers (and believing that everyone is doing a better job than you), supervisors have a tricky task and often undertake this role with relatively little training and often in challenging contexts. The following extract from a chapter that I co-authored provides a good example of what many supervisors are up against.

> 'Are you ready to be a supervisor?' In NHS Talking Therapies settings it's a question that, in our experience, rarely gets asked. Before you have any time to think about it you have been designated a supervisee. The pace of an NHS Talking Therapies service is fast, clinician's caseloads are high; everyone needs

DOI: 10.4324/9781003590620-1

> supervising, at some point everyone will need to 'muck in'. Ideally, you would go on Supervisor Training before you begin supervising, but depending when the training falls, and how many places your service has on the training, you're likely to be asked to supervise without doing it.
>
> (Roscoe & Scullane, 2025, pp. 267–268)

The rollout and rapid expansion of training initiatives such as Improved Access to Psychological Therapies (IAPT) meant that there were relatively few experienced CBT supervisors in relation to the size of the workforce that needed supervision. Consequently, many qualified but relatively inexperienced therapists found themselves supervising very early in their CBT career.

To add to this, CBT training attracts individuals from a wide range of professional backgrounds, some of whom give up their previous role to become a CBT therapist (e.g. mental health nurses) whilst others try to manage acquiring new knowledge and skills alongside the ongoing practise of other therapeutic modalities (e.g. counsellors, clinical psychologists; Rodwell et al., 2023; Wilcockson, 2022). Role transition difficulties have been documented (see Robinson et al., 2012; Wilcockson, 2020); however, there has been little in the way of written guidance to support supervisors in dealing with the intrapersonal conflicts that those new to CBT can face (Roscoe, 2023a). Supervision of Supervision (SoS) which I will refer to later as 'meta-supervision' (Newman, 2013) would seem the most obvious arena for making sense of these challenges yet there is also minimal resources by way of publications or accrediting body guidance on how to structure SoS or what should take place within these sessions (Roscoe, 2020a).

Here come the cavalry

In the United Kingdom (UK), we have seen considerable developments in expert and accrediting body guidelines around the frequency, duration and structure of supervision sessions (e.g. BABCP, 2025; Roth & Pilling, 2008). We have also witnessed the emergence of specific supervision models (e.g. Armstrong & Freeston, 2006), some with an emerging evidence base (Milne & Dunkerley, 2010), and all of these bring much needed theory and practical support to the tasks of supervision.

It is concerning then that the research on routine supervisory practices suggests that these recommendations are often ignored (e.g. Roscoe et al., 2022a). All too often it would seem, supervisors reject these manuals, viewing them as hampering their creativity. Instead, what we see is a picture of supervisors simply talking to their supervisees about their cases (e.g. 'verbal case discussion') rather than working are at a more experiential level (e.g. Spännargård et al., 2025; Townend et al., 2002). This constricted way of supervising does not appear to be limited to those new to the role, suggesting that supervisors do not automatically become more dynamic in their practice with more 'time on the job'. In fact, it might be the opposite whereby qualified therapists are less open to showing their work in supervision, supervisors feel uneasy challenging qualified therapists about their avoidance (in comparison to trainees), thereby reducing the opportunities for skill enhancement (see Liness et al., 2017). The over-reliance on case discussion does not simply hamper the supervisors capacity to make judgements about the competence of their supervisees; it also reduces the opportunities for the supervisee to learn and grow. For example, Bearman et al. (2017) found that trainees who received 'active methods' within supervision demonstrated greater competence than their counterparts who received 'supervision as usual'.

Championing active methods

As a researcher and trainer of supervisors, I have spent the majority of the last decade trying to understand why supervisors and supervisees behave the way they do. Beyond this, I have been working on developing ways to help supervision dyads (a term I shall use as shorthand to refer to the supervisor and supervisee from this point onwards) to move beyond the various sticking points that prevent supervision from being as effective as it could be. This book is the culmination of that work, and ultimately, it is about helping CBT supervisors to make the experience of supervision more active and immersive for their supervisees (and for themselves!). Many of the principles that are described in subsequent chapters are transtheoretical (e.g. they are not specific to Cognitive Therapy and represent the 'pillars' of good quality supervision regardless of the modality); however, the assumption is that the therapy being supervised and delivered is underpinned by Cognitive Therapy (e.g. Beck et al., 1979).

Book structure

The key aim of this book is to provide CBT supervisors with a convincing rationale for making their supervision sessions as active, engaging and immersive as possible. In part I of the book, there is an emphasis on introducing various theories of therapist skill development and in doing so, showing how they can inform and underpin what we do in supervision. Part II provides the foundations for any work that is done in supervision whilst Part III gives examples of how to use a range of active supervision methods. Each chapter will consider questions that supervisors might wish to take to meta-supervision whilst the appendices include considerations for how adaptions can be made for supervision that takes place within a group format.

Bringing these challenges to life

In the chapters that follow, you will see examples of what it is like to supervise therapists in different contexts. The supervision journeys of four fictional supervisees (Basma, Sonny, Tom and Trudie) will showcase how a range of active methods can support their development as CBT therapists.

Basma

Basma has recently changed jobs, having used CBT for eating disorders, and is now working within a National Health Service (NHS) Talking Therapies for Anxiety and Depression (TTAD) service. Basma is less familiar with the formulations and treatment plans for anxiety disorders and depression. Basma is supervised by Ramesh who has been qualified a similar length of time.

Sonny

Sonny is a trainee clinical psychologist who has opted to do a CBT 'pathway' as part of his doctorate. Sonny has previously trained in person centred counselling and reluctantly elected to join the CBT pathway as part of his doctorate due to the belief that having more knowledge and skills in CBT will be advantageous for his future career. Sonny is supervised by a clinical psychologist, Sonia, who works on the clinical psychology programme.

Tom

Tom had worked as a Psychological Wellbeing Practitioner (PWP) within a TTAD service for three years prior to enrolling on a 'high intensity' CBT training course. Tom has access to two supervisors during this time; his university supervisor who he sees as part of a group format with three other trainees and his workplace supervisor, Ramesh.

Trudie

Trudie works as a CBT Therapist in a Child and Adolescent Mental Health (CAMHS) service and has recently finished her CBT training course. Trudie also runs a small private practice in addition to her NHS work. Trudie is also supervised by Sonia, who does not work within the same service as her.

What I have put together is (hopefully) a very practical resource that supervisors and meta-supervisors can 'dip in and out of', as and when they need tips and guidance on how to use a particular method or how to address a specific challenge. All that remains for me to say at this point is that the ideas I present in this book can be seen as the latest iteration of an ongoing 'action research' project (McMahon, 1999) rather than the final product. I hope that it inspires other CBT supervisors to become passionate about active supervision methods and to build on what I outline in this book.

Chapter summary

- Supervisors must balance the need to provide theoretical expertise whilst fostering a safe learning environment for their supervisees.

- Despite guidelines and emerging supervision frameworks, research suggests routine practice often defaults to passive case discussions, limiting skill development.

Recommended reading

Bearman, S. K., Schneiderman, R. L., & Zoloth, E. (2017). Building an evidence base for effective supervision practices: An analogue experiment of supervision to increase EBT fidelity. *Administration and Policy in Mental Health and Mental Health Services Research*, 44, 293–307.

Part I

Reasons to get more active in supervision

Chapter 2

Meeting the needs of your supervisees

Introduction

This is a book about active methods; therefore what better place is there to start than with an experiential exercise about supervision? I invite you to close your eyes and bring to mind any memory you have of being a supervisee. What comes up for you? Is there a standout memory or is there just a generic image of what it is like to be with that supervisor? What emotion or emotions show up? Can you feel any bodily sensations? Is it a positive or negative experience, or perhaps it is fairly neutral?

If you are more fortunate, you might have some positive memories of being supervised to draw upon. If you were able to connect with positive memories of supervision, what were the ingredients that made it so? What desirable characteristics did the supervisor display? What happened in this session that you are recalling to make it memorable, in a good way?

Conversely, if negative memories showed up, what was it about the supervisor's behaviour that contributed to such an experience? What was missing that would have made it a safe or enjoyable experience? Lastly, if you feel indifferent, what was missing and what would need to happen for you to leave supervision feeling more energised and inspired?

It is usually quite easy to recall bad experiences within supervision. In fact, a study by Ellis and colleagues found that from a sample of 363 supervisees, 93% were receiving what was deemed to be 'inadequate' supervision and 35% were receiving 'harmful' supervision (Ellis et al., 2014). A major caveat here is that this was in the United States and the respondents were not CBT therapists, however, given the (often) evaluative nature of supervision, it is not uncommon for people to recall feelings of embarrassment or shame, perhaps linked to comparing yourself to other supervisees and believing that you come up short. In another study involving 128 participants, Ladany et al. (2013) found the highest rated supervisors demonstrated high self-disclosure, interpersonal sensitivity, and there was high levels of agreement on the tasks of supervision. In contrast, the lowest rated supervisors were seen as lacking in technical and interpersonal skills, they rarely included

DOI: 10.4324/9781003590620-3

video or audio observation within sessions and were punitive in the feedback they gave to supervisees.

Active methods as the common denominator?

It is likely that the inclusion or exclusion of active methods is crucial to the emotional reactions in all three of these scenarios. For example, in the negative experiences of supervision camp, there are likely to be recognisable supervisor behaviours that contribute to either inadequate or harmful supervision (Ellis et al., 2014). Table 2.1 highlights some of the most common supervisor behaviours associated with these experiences of supervision. If your memory was of a negative experience, try to see how many of these behaviours resonate with you.

Defining adequate or 'good enough' supervision

Looking at this list of undesirable supervisor behaviours, some are easier to spot than others. For example, it is often very obvious when someone is behaving aggressively, but what is the 'right' amount of cultural humility? How do we judge what an interpersonal process is and is not, and what counts as 'attending to it'? What we are looking to establish here is what a 'good enough' CBT supervisor will do, and it might be as simple as trying to do the opposite of what is known to be ineffective or harmful.

- Focus on helping the supervisee to develop their clinical skills
- Display cultural awareness and humility
- Offer regular and fair feedback
- Address difficulties within the relationship when they arise
- Be warm and open and invite feedback on the effectiveness of their supervision sessions

Table 2.1 Supervisor behaviours associated with ineffective and harmful supervision (based on Ellis et al., 2014)

Supervisor behaviours associated with Ineffective Supervision	*Supervisor behaviours associated with Harmful Supervision*
• Little or no emphasis on skill development • Lacks cultural humility • Fails to provide evaluative feedback • Fails to address interpersonal processes within the supervisory relationship • Is cold and distant • Does not listen to the supervisee	• Behaves in an aggressive or abusive manner • Behaves in a sexually inappropriate manner • Feedback is cruel

Supervisor tip

As a supervisor, you will need to give your supervisees feedback that might be difficult for them to take at times, invoking feelings of anxiety and shame. This is unavoidable given that gatekeeping and quality assurance are essential (Bernard & Goodyear, 2014). For example, inviting a supervisee to engage in a role-play exercise can generate difficult emotions yet it is done with the intention of aiding their learning and development. The way that the feedback is delivered will determine whether it is effective, ineffective or harmful.

Understanding the mechanisms that drive supervision

Offering adequate supervision means that we need to provide an environment where supervisees can feel safe but also where they can develop their skills as therapists. Milne and Dunkerley (2010) use a tandem bike analogy to explain how effective supervision works. The front wheel represents the behaviours of the supervisor and the rear wheel represents the supervisee's learning, framed within Kolb's learning cycle (Kolb, 1984). Milne and colleagues also developed the Supervision Adherence and Guidance Evaluation (SAGE) instrument (Milne & Reiser, 2014) which can be used to measure the degree to which these processes are present in any given supervision session, together with a number of 'common factors' (e.g. 'collaborating').

Figure 2.1 provides a visual representation of the hypothesed supervision processes, methods and specific supervisory skills that are likely to underpin adequate supervision. For example, in order to initiate the process of experiential learning (e.g. taking the supervisee around Kolb's learning cycle), a specific *method* that is most likely to achieve this aim must be selected. If we consider a role-play task whereby the supervisee experiences what it is like to be the client, the supervisor must them deploy certain *skills* to ensure that the supervisee reflects on the task (e.g. generates affect and reflection; Milne & Reiser, 2014). What is clear from this is that a conversation alone is unlikely to facilitate this *process*. Active methods are therefore the driving force behind effective supervisee learning.

Establishing your active methods baseline

Before reading the rest of the book, it would be useful to consider where you are starting from in terms of your use of active methods. Firstly, it is probably helpful to explain what is meant by 'active'. Rather than viewing supervision as either active or inactive, we might think of it as a continuum of activity (see Figure 2.2).

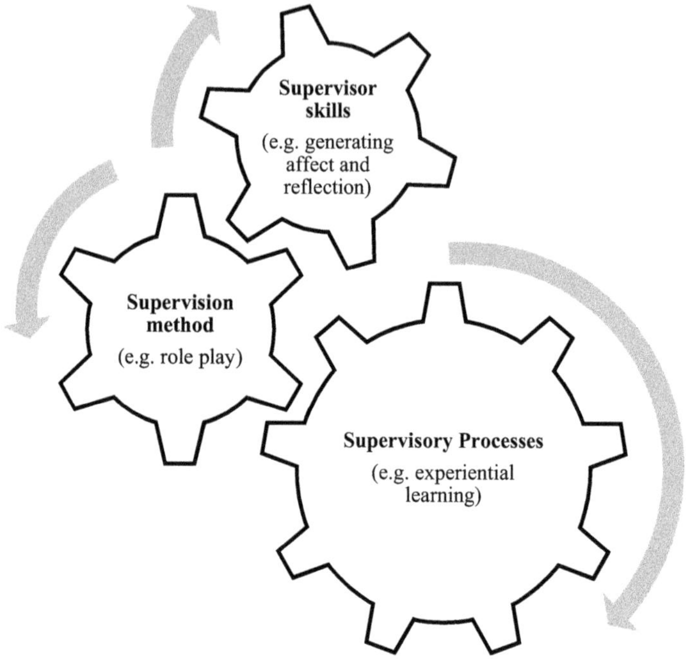

Figure 2.1 The interplay between supervisory skills, methods and processes.

Passive					Immersive
Advice giving / advice seeking Recommending papers / book chapters to read	Supervisor modelling Reviewing session recordings without a clear supervision question	Writing out formulations Skills rehearsal Reviewing session recordings linked to a specific skill domain	Deliberate Practice Salient Circles Exercise	Self-Practice of CBT methods Completing questionnaires (e.g. Therapist schemas; Alignment to CBT scale)	Chair work Behavioural Experiments
Didactic					**Guided Discovery**
Affect likely to be lower					**Affect likely to be higher**

Figure 2.2 Active methods continuum.

Style

This continuum is characterised by the style of the supervisor, with them behaving in a more didactic fashion at the lower end and using more Socratic Dialogue at the other (Padesky, 1993). At one end of the continuum we have supervision methods that are fairly passive forms of learning (e.g. the supervisee sits and listens to the supervisor who dispenses their clinical wisdom through instructions or anecdotes). For example, verbal case discussion can be considered as being an exchange of information between supervisor and supervisee that consists of two elements – *providing details about a case* and *giving instruction.* In other words, advice seeking and advice giving. The supervisor is acting in a more didactic manner and from a supervisee learning perspective, this is a passive process whereby they are a receptable for the knowledge that the supervisor dispenses.

Activities

Next, we have activities such as when the supervisor models how to draw out a formulation or how to deliver an intervention. In this instance, the supervisor is active, but the supervisee is still quite passive in terms of their engagement. We could ask a supervisee to draw out a formulation which makes their role more active, but it is not especially immersive. This is where the concept of 'head versus heart' learning comes into play, whereby a concept is understood intellectually but not emotionally (Grant et al., 2008).

Role-play, where the supervisee steps into the shoes of their client is a more immersive experience, as they are often gaining a deeper appreciation of the emotions of their client (Pugh & Margetts, 2020). This can increase empathy and help them to experience what it feels like to be asked certain questions or to engage in a CBT exercise. At the upper end of the continuum, we have activities that are likely to generate the most emotion within the supervisee and therefore have the potential for the deepest learning. Conducting CBT on oneself (e.g. taking part in a thought-action fusion experiment) or engaging in chair work are good examples of high affect-high immersion. An activity such as chair work is more immersive as the supervisee is physically active (e.g. moving chairs) and they are embodying different perspectives (that of other parts of them or the minds or emotions of others such as their clients). In these activities, the supervisor is less of a 'teacher' and more a 'facilitator' (Pugh, 2019).

The functions of case discussion

Case Discussion (CD) is perhaps the most widely used method whereby the supervisor relies upon the supervisee to provide information about differential diagnosis, choice of formulation, intervention selection and sequencing or challenges within the client-therapist relationship. To draw upon an old saying, no one is proposing that we 'throw the baby out with the bathwater'. Instead, what we need to do is understand the function of case discussion before deciding its merits in any given situation. For example, an over-reliance on case discussion could relate to a supervisor lacking the confidence to use active methods (Pugh & Margetts, 2020) or it could stem from perpetual supervisee avoidance of any activities that make them uncomfortable.

The Beliefs about Supervision Scale (BASS-12; see Appendix 4) is a twelve-item reflective tool that has been developed with the intention of helping supervisors to reflect upon attitudes towards various aspects of supervision. Completing this might enable you to better understand your relationship with active methods and how this in turn, influences your response to your supervisees attitudes towards them. At this point in time, the BASS-12 has not undergone any form of official validation as a measure. Items have been generated by sending a list of beliefs to a small number of highly experienced supervisors. It contains statements that reveal certain assumptions about supervision, the role of a supervisor and their relationship with their supervisees.

Whilst there are no right or wrong answers per se, there might be several unintended consequences of holding some of these attitudes tightly. For example, believing strongly that Self-Practice/Self-Reflection (SP/SR; Bennett-Levy et al., 2014) has no place in supervision could mean that a supervisor misses out on many opportunities to help their supervisees tap into this avenue of skill building.

Assessing your active methods baseline

The final part of this chapter invites you to consider the frequency in which you incorporate various active methods into your supervision sessions. The aim of Table 2.2 is to help you to reflect on which ones you use most of the time, which ones only some of the time and which ones you never use. After you have completed the checklist, I would invite you to consider the reasons why some feature more often than others. As you read the other chapters in the book, you might start to gain a better understanding of what has shaped and is continuing to shape your behaviour as a supervisor. I hope that what follows will give you confidence to expand your supervisory repertoire and move you towards being a more dynamic CBT supervisor.

In Chapter 1, four supervisees were mentioned, and here, their supervisors Ramesh and Sonia are introduced as they seek to reflect on their active methods baseline.

> Ramesh was able to see that he regularly asks his supervisees to bring video or audio recordings and that he helps them to track outcome measures as a way of considering client progress. He noticed that he rarely asked his supervisees to make their supervision questions specific therefore set himself a goal of asking for this over the next month. Ramesh was also unfamiliar with chair work as it had not been part of his therapy training.
>
> In contrast, Sonia reflected that she was quite consistent at maintaining the structure of supervision yet often neglects outcome measures and does not ask her supervisees to bring recordings on a regular basis.

Table 2.2 Active methods checklist

Supervisory task	*Every time*	*Monthly*	*Twice a year*	*Once a year*	*Never*
I ask my supervisees to prepare specific supervision questions					
I ask my supervisees to regularly bring video or audio clips					
I set my supervisees homework tasks					
I model how to develop formulations or how to deliver an intervention					
I ask my supervisee to re-enact a scenario with a client and develop a role-play task to support their learning					
I help my supervisees to review outcomes measures as a way of monitoring client progress					
I help supervisees to spot their own problematic beliefs that impact on their therapy or supervisory relationships					
I utilise perspective taking through the use of chair work					
I encourage my supervisees to use CBT methods on themselves					

Questions for meta-supervision

Ramesh and Sonia might decide to take their active methods checklist to their meta-supervisor to help them reflect on the factors that are perpetuating the underutilisation of certain methods within their own supervision.

Reflecting on your own use of use active methods, what might you want to explore with your meta-supervisor?

Chapter summary

- Adequate supervision involves a combination of focusing on skill development, cultural humility, and creating opportunities for regular and constructive feedback.
- Effective CBT supervisors actively address relational difficulties and work to create a warm, collaborative environment.
- Effective supervision balances safety and experiential learning, requiring active engagement beyond conversation. Supervisors should expand their repertoire to include immersive methods for deeper learning and cultural competence.

- Active methods are essential for experiential learning and deeper skill acquisition. Passive approaches (e.g. advice-giving, case discussion) are less effective compared to immersive techniques like role-play, chair work, and self-practice of CBT methods.
- There is also an active Methods FAQs page at the end of the book (see Appendix 1).

Recommended reading

Ellis, M. V., Berger, L., Hanus, A. E., Ayala, E. E., Swords, B. A., & Siembor, M. (2014). Inadequate and harmful clinical supervision: Testing a revised framework and assessing occurrence. *The Counseling Psychologist*, 42(4), 434–472.

Chapter 3

Core functions of supervision

Introduction

What is supervision and how does it differ from other forms of support that are available to CBT therapists? The answer is not as straight forward as one might imagine, given that the NHS Talking Therapies for Anxiety and Depression (TTAD) manual (National Collaborating Centre for Mental Health, 2019) identifies six different types of supervision.

- Clinical case management supervision
- Line management supervision
- Clinical skills supervision
- Meta-supervision
- Peer supervision
- Reflective practice/supervision

Detailed descriptions of how these supervision formats differ from one another is not provided within the TTAD manual, although case management and line management would appear to be very similar. For those that do work in NHS settings, the boundaries between these different types of supervision can become blurred. For example, in certain contexts, or when supervision 'drifts' (Roscoe, 2021b) the content and structure of clinical supervision might sometimes resemble case management.

Clinical skills supervision

The overall focus of clinical skills supervision is to help the supervisee to develop and retain competence in the application of various CBT formulations and interventions for a range of mental health problems for which CBT has been shown to be effective (e.g. Butler et al., 2006). As this book is written for CBT supervisors working across a range of contexts, some of which are outside of the NHS, Case Management (CM) Supervision will not be a feature for the remainder of the book, except as a reference point for understanding prior beliefs about supervision.

DOI: 10.4324/9781003590620-4

Bernard and Goodyear (2014) offer a useful summary of the distinct nature of clinical (skills) supervision stating that:

> This relationship is evaluative and hierarchical, extends over time, and has the simultaneous purposes of enhancing the professional functioning of the more junior person(s); monitoring the quality of professional services offered to the clients, she, he, or they see; and serving as a gatekeeper for the particular profession the supervisee seeks to enter.
>
> (p 9)

The work of Derek Milne and colleagues has also been instrumental in advancing our understanding of clinical supervision, helping to provide more specificity and drawing attention to certain characteristics that make it distinct from these other activities (Milne & Watkins, 2014). For example, the educative basis has been emphasised and the use of corrective feedback and goal setting. Pilling and Roth (2014) also point to the inclusion of a contract which is often not included in CM supervision.

Whichever modality of supervision you are providing (e.g. CBT or person-centred counselling), there are certain 'core functions' that underpin your role, and these functions should determine how you spend the time with your supervisee in each session. These functions are typically referred to as normative (managerial), formative (educative) and restorative (supportive) duties (Proctor, 1994). More commonly, the three supervisory functions overlap, with two or more needing to be addressed simultaneously (see Figure 3.1).

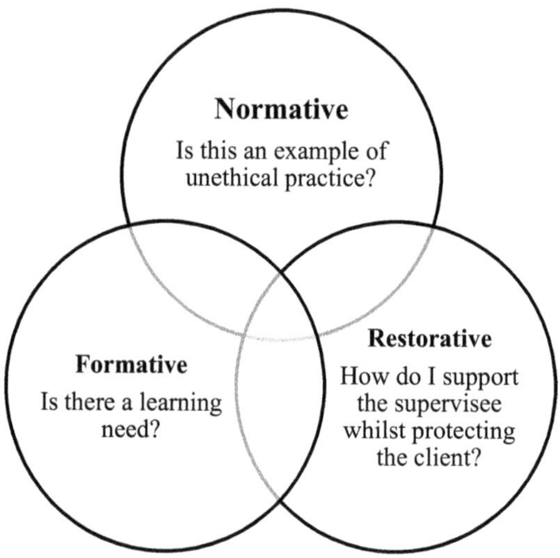

Figure 3.1 Overlapping functions of supervision.

There are some key words related to Bernard and Goodyear's definition of supervision which help us to understand how these core functions are operationalised by supervisors. First, the idea that supervision is *evaluative*. Anecdotal evidence would suggest that the majority of supervisors feel most comfortable attending to the formative duties as this mirrors many of the skills that are used in therapy (e.g. educating the client about the maintenance of their problems and teaching them skills to help improve their symptoms). Furthermore, this is often where supervision feels the most rewarding when we see clear improvements in the skills and confidence of our supervisees. In contrast, evaluating the supervisee can generate concerns about how this might affect their confidence or the strength of the supervisory relationship. Indeed, the normative and restorative domains can generate numerous challenges for CBT supervisors. For example:

At what point do we need to intervene when there are ethical concerns about the supervisee's clinical practice?

When does attending to the emotional needs of the supervisee stray into the territory of personal therapy?

> Having previously experienced social anxiety, Tom dreaded the idea of having to do 'bandwidth broadening' experiments as part of training such as deliberately doing something 'silly' in public to gauge how others respond. When Tom brought a social anxiety case to supervision, his supervisor Ramesh suspected that he was avoiding certain aspects because of his own anxiety. Ramesh had to hold in mind that by only doing parts of the treatment protocol, Tom was not providing his client with access to the evidence-based treatment. This raised ethical concerns. Ramesh also needed to consider if Tom fully understand the rationale for why certain interventions were central to the effectiveness of the protocol. Finally, Ramesh also needed to consider how emotionally challenging it is for Tom to work with social anxiety given his lived experience of the problem.

Understandably, normative and formative functions are paramount when supporting novice therapists, yet it is crucial that we do not become complacent in these areas when supervising experienced therapists (Roscoe & Scullane, 2025).

> Trudie would frequently attend supervision without any clear supervision questions and proceeded to 'offload' about how challenging it was to maintain her dual roles as case manager and therapist. Despite her attempts to establish structure from the start of their relationship, Sonia found it difficult to attend to her formative and normative duties. Trudie would leave supervision saying that she felt better for 'getting it off her chest' however, it was unclear what learning was taking place.

Another important word in Bernard and Goodyear's description is *hierarchical*, which implies that the supervisor occupies a position of authority or seniority either through job title or level of experience. There is often a greater power imbalance between supervisor and supervisee than therapist and client as De Stefano et al. (2017) put it 'supervisees, unlike clients who can opt out of treatment, often do not have the option of discontinuing supervision or switching to a different supervisor when they feel that they are not getting what they need from supervision' (p 224). This is particularly true during training and within statutory services (e.g. NHS), meaning that therapists in private practice (PP) have more power to leave if they are not satisfied. Power can be associated with a whole host of problems and often supervisors will struggle with managing their role power regardless of context, either by trying to avoid it or, worse, misusing it (Hawkins & Shohet, 2000). Classical hierarchical relationships are seen in the supervisor-supervisee dynamic during training courses, however the popularity of peer supervision arrangements amongst qualified therapists means that there is the risk that no one is 'in charge' of monitoring normative, formative and restorative functions.

Gatekeeping

In some instances, where the supervisor has major concerns about certain aspects of a supervisee's competence there is a need to act as a 'gatekeeper' to the profession (e.g. where their actions impact upon client safety) using 'legitimate power' (Holloway, 1995) to report their concerns to course tutors, or in extreme cases, to approach an organisation that regulates the practice of the individual (e.g. the BABCP).

> **Supervisor tip**
>
> Post-qualification, it is unlikely that there will be such a strong focus on normative functions especially in PP, where the supervisor is often chosen by the supervisee and has no managerial 'power' to wield. Supervisors need to be mindful of some supervisees 'competing' with them over who has more knowledge and skills.

Cultural competency

The development of cultural humility (CH) and cultural responsiveness (CR) are seen as ways to build cultural competence and have become increasingly recognised as core skills for therapists (Naeem et al., 2019). Supervisors are well positioned to model CR and CH and to assist supervisees in developing these skills. This is also likely to involve normative, formative and restorative overlaps. For example, white supervisees (and white supervisors) are likely to need ongoing formative support in supervision or meta-supervision to ensure that they work and think inclusively (see Vekaria et al., 2023). Conversely, supervisees from minoritised groups may benefit from restorative discussions, especially when there are large scale events that trigger difficult thoughts and feelings (e.g. war, terrorism, high profile media cases).

Maintaining the right balance

Attending to the normative, formative and restorative demands of supervision can often feel like a juggling act. Consequently, restorative needs can sometimes be overshadowed by the demands for ethical adherence and the development of therapist competence. Where supervision time is already precious and in short supply, and in contexts where 'recovery rates' and service throughput are prioritised (Painter, 2018), this can lead to very limiting beliefs amongst both supervisors and supervisees about the scope of supervision. For example, in a study that I conducted with trainee CBT therapists (Roscoe, 2021a), it was found that supervisees were willing to expand their use of supervision (e.g. the types of questions that they brought to supervision) if they received training on topics such as interpersonal processes (IP). In other words, they did not realise that IP could be discussed within CBT supervision until permission was given to do so. This shows how attitudes arising from the macro (national curriculums) and micro cultures (place of employment) in which CBT is practised, can contribute towards constricted use of supervision.

Reflective exercise

Think about one person that you currently supervise or have done so in the past.
Was there an even balance between the three functions?
If the balance was uneven, why was this?
What might the unintended consequences be of maintaining this imbalance?

Making appropriate adaptations

Increasing recognition of neurodiversity amongst therapists (Lewis, 2024; Taylor & Sims, 2025) also signals a need to consider how training environments are often set up for the neurotypical, meaning a higher level of stress in what is already a highly stressful time (Bennett-Levy & Beedie, 2007). Appropriate adaptions are sensible and necessary within supervision; however, some supervisors can place too much emphasis on what I describe as 'restorative-lite' duties such as allowing supervisees to offload in an unfocused way or colluding with them about service pressures at the expense of considering learning needs. Self-Practice/Self-Reflection (SP/SR) is a structured, CBT congruent approach to understanding how our 'personal self' influences and is influenced by our 'therapist self'. Supervisors can use SP/SR to address the restorative aspects of supervision in a meaningful way. Recent developments include an SP/SR programme dedicated to supporting therapists from ethnically minority backgrounds (Chowdhury et al., 2025).

Helping trainees adapt to CBT supervision

The degree to which a supervisor will undertake each of these core functions also varies considerably depending on the context (e.g. private practice or NHS), the developmental stage of the supervisee (see Stoltenberg & McNeill, 2010) and the relationship between supervisor and supervisee. The style, content and focus of supervision within psychotherapy may be very different to supervision that individuals have been exposed to previously. For example, Psychological Wellbeing Practitioners (PWPs) might be more familiar with exploring the normative aspects within CM Supervision and find the restorative element a welcome addition (Painter, 2018). Conversely, the ongoing educative focus within supervision might differ considerably between therapeutic modalities (e.g. CBT versus Psychodynamic). For example, there might have been more or less of a focus on self-reflection in previous roles, more or less of a focus on client throughput and scores on outcome measures. One of the key differences is that psychotherapy training often requires supervisees to bring video recordings of therapy sessions which can feel threatening if they have never had to do this before. In summary, there will most likely be cultural or contextual differences for CBT trainees and they are likely to need specific support in adjusting to changes in normative, formative or restorative domains.

Questions for meta-supervision

Am I striking the right balance between focusing on normative, formative and restorative functions?

If applicable, what factors are leading to an imbalance?

Chapter summary

- Supervisors need to undertake normative, formative and restorative duties and the emphasis on each will vary depending on the context, stage of supervisee skill development and agreed goals.
- Many supervisors enjoy the formative and restorative aspects of supervision yet struggle with the normative elements. It can feel uncomfortable giving feedback on a supervisee's skills when they are underperforming and is not always well

received. At times, this can have implications for another persons' career which does not sit well with most supervisors. Supervisors also need to ensure that restorative supervision does not become just a 'cosy chat'.

- Supervisors should be mindful of the need to include restorative discussions and exercises as an integral part of their work. For example, a supervisor can help their supervisee to evaluate their emotional responses to clinical work, monitoring for signs of possible 'burnout' or counter-transference reactions. This could also include helping them to notice any urges to avoid key aspects of CBT.

Recommended reading

Proctor, B. (1994). Supervision – competence, confidence, accountability. *British Journal of Guidance & Counselling*, 22, 309–318.

Chapter 4

CBT supervision

Distinctive features

Introduction

One of the most distinctive features of CBT is its alignment with evidence-based practice (EBP) therefore CBT supervision has a strong emphasis on monitoring adherence to evidenced based models and treatment plans (Roth et al., 2010). Afterall, CBT has achieved its place at the 'top of the table' (e.g. being the first line approach for many disorders; see NICE, 2005, 2009, 2011, 2013, 2014, 2018) by demonstrating its outcomes in randomised control trials (RCTs; Butler et al., 2006). During these RCTs, a manualised approach is used to ensure that therapists are delivering the same treatment to different clients, otherwise it would be difficult to reliably measure the impact of the interventions (Kazantzis, 2003; Roth et al., 2010). This chapter will consider how CBT supervisors can support both new and experienced therapists in maintaining 'fidelity' to the theoretical underpinnings and interventions that are used across CBT, whilst addressing some of the challenges that come with this.

Treatment and model fidelity

Often RCT manuals include specific techniques, a specific formulation template (e.g. Ehlers & Clark, 2000) and a specific order in which techniques are used (e.g. Fairburn, 2008). What is also distinct about RCT's is the level of supervisory input. Trial-based therapists often receive more frequent supervision in comparison to those in routine settings (Townend et al., 2002), their behaviour with their clients is often more closely monitored (e.g. reviewing video recordings of therapy sessions; Spännargård et al., 2025) and the effectiveness of what they are doing session by session is tracked carefully (e.g. using weekly outcome measures; Barkham et al., 2023). Furthermore, those providing supervision have usually developed the manual or have expertise in the treatment of the problem.

Adherence and competence

In order to replicate the results that are achieved in RCTs, it is necessary for CBT supervisors to monitor the degree to which their supervisees deliver CBT as

DOI: 10.4324/9781003590620-5

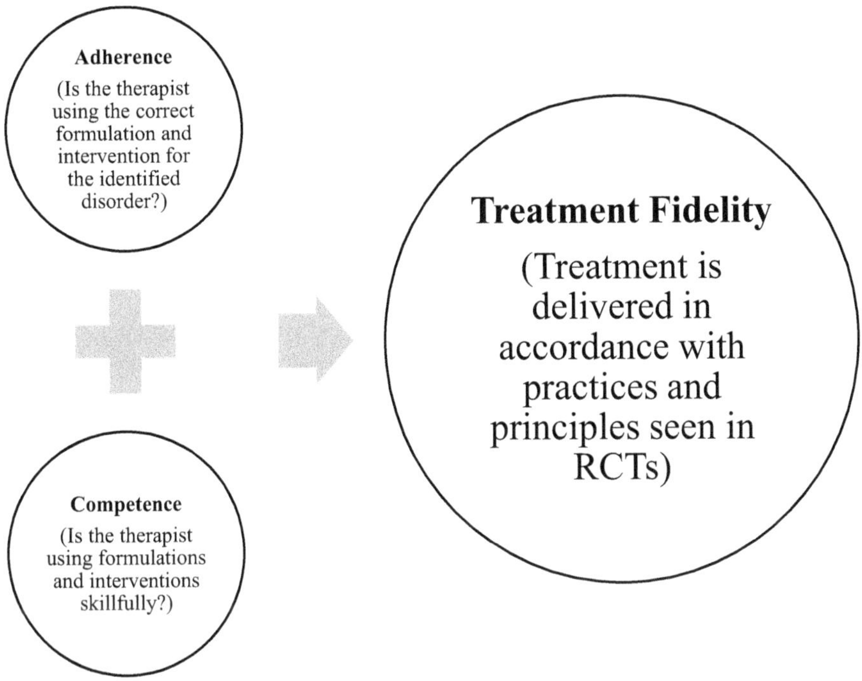

Figure 4.1 The components of treatment fidelity.

intended (Kazantzis, 2003). CBT supervisors often focus on two aspects of treatment 'fidelity' – therapist adherence (TA) and therapist competence (TC) to determine if therapy is being delivered in accordance with the most appropriate protocol for the client's presenting problems (see Figure 4.1).

Adherence

Adherence occurs when the therapist selects the correct formulation or interventions however, this is only one part of the treatment equation. A therapist might deliver the correct intervention but does so in a way that makes it ineffective. For example, a therapist might ask a client to relive a traumatic memory in the context of a Post Traumatic Stress Disorder (PTSD) diagnosis but fail to deliver the intervention adequately (e.g. does not update any of the hotspots). As Barton and Armstrong (2018) put it 'therapists can be adherent but not competent, competent but not adherent, or both adherent and competent' (p 41). Overall, the research on the link between TA, TC and client outcomes is mixed, however, Haug et al. (2016) found that lower TA and TC was associated with higher dropout rates amongst socially anxious clients. Meanwhile, greater TA and TC was associated with better outcomes for those with panic disorder.

Reflective exercise

How much importance do you place on treatment fidelity?
How does this influence the content of your supervision sessions?

Model selection

The first step in trying to replicate 'RCT level' therapy is ensuring that the model selected by the therapist fits the diagnosis. Where trial therapists often carefully determine diagnostic specificity through use of diagnostic interviews that are faithful to Diagnostic and Statistical Manual (DSM) criteria (American Psychiatric Association, 2013), many CBT therapists are told during their training that they 'do not diagnose'. Instead, they use routine outcome measures (ROMS) to determine the presence of a disorder or the primary treatment target (Clark, 2011). The reliability of this method of assessment has been questioned (Scott, 2020) however, there are also times when the problem that the client presents with does not fit neatly within diagnostic categories. In these instances, there is not always a model that has been tested via an RCT to check for adherence. This means that a 'best fit' model is sometimes selected that uses either transdiagnostic techniques (e.g. cognitive restructuring) or helps to simplify co-morbid problems (e.g. Fennell, 1997). Salkovskis et al. (2023) highlight how various forms of evidence-based practice can inform our work as CBT therapists in the absence of an RCT. For example, we can draw upon the findings of single case designs that provide treatment plans or formulations that are faithful to the generic CBT model.

> Trudie is often contacted by private clients who do not meet diagnostic criteria for a diagnosable mental health disorder. An example of this is some of the clients she has treated for relationship jealousy. There is no NICE guidance for this problem and no RCT has been developed thus far. Trudie uses the Leahy book that offers a CBT approach for overcoming jealousy.
>
> (see Leahy, 2018)

Competence

Whilst adherence is relatively straight forward to determine (e.g. the supervisee is following a Panic Disorder protocol), establishing whether competence has been attained is fraught with difficulties (Muse et al., 2022). For example, is competence something that is binary, static and generalisable or does it fluctuate based on the nature of the presenting problem and the context in which therapy takes place?

> Tom had achieved a pass mark for his first video submission as part of his CBT training course; a treatment session of a depressed client. However, Ramesh was

doubtful that Tom would pass if he was to submit a session for a client with an anxiety disorder at this stage in his training.

Basma had demonstrated competence by passing three video submissions during her training, however, Ramesh had concerns about Basma retaining fidelity to the model now that she is qualified and when she is not being observed.

What these experiences highlight is that measuring competence periodically can fail to show the 'full picture' of the enduring skilfulness of a CBT therapist. Indeed Muse et al. (2022) suggest that trainers and supervisors should apply caution when making judgements about competence especially when relying on a single measure such as the Cognitive Therapy Scale Revised (CTS-R; Blackburn et al., 2001).

One can learn to 'play the game' for the cameras or cherry pick good quality sessions that are not representative of a person's general therapeutic skills. Furthermore, there are situations in which a therapist must draw upon 'meta-competencies' to deal with nuances in clinical presentations which mean that some items on scales might not be endorsed despite high quality CBT being on display (Campbell-Lee et al., 2024).

Measuring competence

Nevertheless, some of the normative and formative aspects of CBT supervision are usually addressed using competence measures. UK based supervisors are likely to have some familiarity with the CTS-R (Blackburn et al., 2001), an updated version of the Cognitive Therapy Scale (CTS; Young & Beck, 1980). The CTS-R is commonly used within TTAD training courses and for assessing the CBT component of Clinical Psychology training (BABCP, 2025). For those less familiar with the CTS-R, it assesses generic CBT skills that would be expected to be seen in any CBT treatment session. Variants have been developed to be more applicable to specific disorders (e.g. Haddock et al., 2001) but retain similar features such as rating each skill from zero to six.

Detecting and learning from strengths and weaknesses

Learning from the feedback that is given after CTS-R assessment is often seen in supervisees strengthening their skills in areas where they were previously weak and scoring higher on future submissions. Liness et al. (2019) found that competence as determined by a CTS-R pass mark was sustained following training, however, there was no significant link between therapist competence and patient outcomes. This study also found a concerning trend that once qualified, many CBT therapists stopped showing recordings of their clinical work within supervision. Of note, an earlier study by Shaw et al. (1999) found that the only items that were associated with patient outcomes on the CTS (Young & Beck, 1980) were agenda setting, pacing and homework setting. It would make sense that supervisors help their supervisees to retain or improve competence in at least these three areas once qualified, yet case discussion alone might fail to highlight skill deficits in these areas.

Assessing competence in 'Real-world' therapy

Many therapists are known to be sceptical about RCTs and how applicable disorder-specific models are to their own work with clients (Moloney & Kelly, 2004). The context in which therapy takes place is likely to shape the 'version' of CBT that is provided. For example, those in PP have more flexibility in how they work, compared to those in NHS settings. The CBT supervisor must hold in mind the context and client population when considering if their supervisees are demonstrating fidelity to the generic CBT model.

> In her NHS role, Trudie is restricted to offering 12 sessions and forbidden from using more transdiagnostic CBT models such as Low Self Esteem and Perfectionism because they do not match with a specific disorder. In her Private Practice, Trudie uses these models as many of her clients do not neatly fit with the disorder specific models or show limited improvement. Trudie is also able to work for a longer period of time with clients, basing treatment duration on each presentation.

Phased and augmented treatment plans

Phased and/or augmented treatment can work well when it is justified by a formulation (e.g. Birdsey, 2020) however, therapist drift is a major concern within CBT, whereby clinicians knowingly or unknowingly fail to implement core ingredients that make a treatment more likely to be successful (Waller, 2009). A thorough examination of the pros and cons of taking a phased or augmented approach to treatment is beyond the scope of this chapter, however, some of the challenges brought about by these will feature in later chapters. Of note, some therapists can end up applying a 'mix and match' approach to treatment which is different from this and can be a cause for concern (Ledley et al., 2011). To use a cake analogy, you can change some of the ingredients but if you take the main ones or too many away, you no longer have a cake. If you just use ingredients at random, you don't really have a sense of what it is that you are trying to make in the first place.

Supervisor tip

It is prudent for supervisors to explore therapist approaches during the contracting phase and to anticipate where there might be a need to consider multi-modality supervision. For qualified supervisees, agreeing whether supervision is purely CBT focused or is to include other approaches (e.g. Eye Movement Desensitisation and Reprocessing; EMDR) is essential. For trainees, it is important to consider how previous ways of working (e.g. if they have been a counsellor prior to CBT training) may need to be phased out or 'put on hold' whilst they try to gain competence in CBT.

Keeping an eye on treatment fidelity

As an evidence-based therapy, it is important that CBT practitioners endeavour to provide their clients with the treatments that have been shown to work in RCTs, and which feature in clinical implementation guidelines (e.g. NICE, 2009). CBT supervisors should support their supervisees to maintain fidelity to the generic cognitive model wherever possible. This includes considerations around the choice of treatment protocols, when to consider a phase-based treatment or when to augment CBT with compatible formulations and interventions. Adherence to treatment is not simply a matter of therapist preference, it is also a matter of ethics (Hope, 2010). An occupational hazard of being a therapist is the risk of being summoned to a coroners court and once there, rationales for decisions that were made during treatment must be justified. For this reason, we as supervisors always need to keep a metaphorical eye on the normative not just formative and restorative functions of supervision.

Questions for meta-supervision

How do I ensure that my supervisees are maintaining fidelity to the overall principles and practices that are shown to make CBT effective?

My supervisee and I hold similar negative beliefs about protocols, how might this impact on my judgment?

Chapter summary

- Monitoring and supporting treatment adherence underpin CBT supervision.
- It is important that those providing CBT supervision are aware of their own beliefs about CBT and are able to anticipate how and when this might become a problem within supervision.
- Clinical Psychologists are trained to work in a more integrative manner whilst some CBT therapists take a phased approach, using EMDR to target some aspects of a client's presenting problems and CBT for other aspects of treatment. Others will 'bolt on' standalone interventions from third wave therapies (e.g. values work) or focus on developing self-compassion to augment the CBT

treatment for Depression in those who are highly self-critical. Supervisors should consider whether separate supervision is needed for phased approaches to treatment and if they have the skills to support augmentation.

- In cases where there is no evidence-based model (e.g. relationship jealousy), adherence to general CBT principles and competence in their application would be considered as demonstrating overall fidelity.

Recommended reading

Kendall, P. C., & Frank, H. E. (2018). Implementing evidence-based treatment protocols: Flexibility within fidelity. *Clinical Psychology: Science and Practice*, 25(4), 40.

Chapter 5

Understanding therapist skill development

Introduction

Becoming competent in the practice of CBT is a career long commitment rather than a final destination. Individuals such as Basma, Sonny, Tom and Trudie commence CBT training with different strengths and weaknesses and, to use an athletics track analogy, it is important that supervisors understand that supervisees start from different positions in different domains, rather than all needing the same level of support at the same time. For example, Sonny's interpersonal skills were more advanced than some of his peers due to him having worked as a counsellor in the past, whilst Tom's knowledge of TTAD services (and having worked as a Psychological Wellbeing Practitioner; PWP) meant that his CBT skills were more advanced in some areas than Sonny. Similarly, qualified therapists will be more confident and competent in some areas than others. This chapter will briefly introduce one of the most influential models of therapist skill development, the Declarative-Procedural-Reflective (DPR) model (Bennett-Levy, 2006, 2019) and consider how this can guide the work of CBT supervisors when supporting novices and highly experienced therapists.

The DPR model

The DPR model (Bennett-Levy, 2006) provides a theoretical framework for understanding the building blocks of therapist skill development. Despite the number of times it has been cited in other publications, my experience of interacting with supervisors during training workshops suggests that most have not heard of it and for those that have, it rarely informs their work within supervision. This is unfortunate as the DPR model provides a relatively simple yet robust basis for our selection of supervisory methods at any given time.

In a nutshell, the model proposes that therapists learn and continue to develop through three interacting components: Declarative knowledge, Procedural skills and the Reflective system. Each component of the model is associated with typical modes of learning (Bennett-Levy et al., 2009) and supervisors can reinforce the skills that are being acquired from classroom teaching, group work and clinical interactions (see Table 5.1). For example, those new to CBT will acquire facts and theoretical

DOI: 10.4324/9781003590620-6

Table 5.1 Using the DPR to inform supervisory input

DPR Component	*Typical mode of learning*	*Supervisory Input*
Declarative Knowledge (e.g. knowing what the Clark (1986) Panic model looks like, understanding its parts and how it is maintained)	Tutor explains model, describes examples of model and how it informs treatment Reading key publications	Provides more contextual, nuanced examples. Directs supervisees to wider reading materials.
Procedural Skills (e.g. ability to implement CBT techniques in line with formulations and in response to client presentation)	Tutor modelling Role-play with other trainees	Supervisor modelling to help expand on classroom examples Role-play between Supervisor and Supervisee Deliberate Practice Providing feedback on procedural skills observed during video clip
Reflective System (e.g. drawing on declarative and procedural systems to consider solutions to obstacles that arise during treatment)	Self-reflective exercises Self-Practice/Self Reflection (SP/SR; Bennett-Levy et al., 2014)	Administering questionnaires such as the Therapist Schema Questionnaire (Leahy, 2001) Using Chair work to help supervisee adopt the perspective of their client Undertaking a behavioural experiment within supervision

knowledge about formulations, interventions, treatment protocols and how to engage clients in therapy. This 'declarative knowledge' (DK) is usually acquired through attending lectures or reading books and journal papers. Johnston and Milne (2012) found that early-stage trainees needed a greater degree of educational scaffolding therefore CBT supervisors can support the development of DK by clarifying any misunderstanding during supervision or through suggesting further reading.

Technical and conceptual skills

Knowing about a topic or even how to deliver an intervention does not automatically guarantee that one can execute this skill in clinical practice. The framework developed by Miller (1990) compliments the DPR by breaking the knowledge to skill transition down into a series of steps. The following example uses longitudinal formulation as the basis for observing the progression from knowing about a topic at an intellectual or 'head level' through to being able to demonstrate this in their clinical work.

Knows – understands what a formulation is and its intended purpose
Knows how – can describe how a formulation is written and presented to a client

Shows how – can demonstrate this skill during a role- play exercise
Does – implements the skill with a real client (e.g. submits video recording evidencing this)

We can think of the 'knows' and 'knows how' as the acquisition of 'declarative knowledge'. Therapists begin their training with a broad range of facts and knowledge about generic aspects of mental health support (e.g. what Roth and Pilling (2007) describe as 'generic competences). Some will already have conceptual knowledge of certain elements of CBT (e.g. former PWPs such as Tom are accustomed to using 'low intensity' CBT interventions). Others like Sonny, may have less declarative knowledge and sometimes hold negative beliefs about CBT (e.g. that is easy to learn or does not address 'the root of the problem').

Reflective exercise

Consider a supervisee past or present. How would you assess their level of declarative knowledge and/or procedural skills?

Using supervision to consolidate declarative knowledge

Supervision provides supervisees like Tom and Sonny with ample opportunities to cement or update their technical or conceptual knowledge and skills by revisiting their understanding of theoretical concepts they have learned about in lectures or other teaching sessions. Supervision is also an optimal environment to sharpen technical skills by observing the supervisor through modelling or practising skills via role- play.

> Having attended one lecture on the topic, Tom was still unclear about what constituted Panic Disorder. He was still working towards the 'knows' aspect of skill development. His supervisor (Ramesh) helped Tom to understand the difference between panic attacks that are cued by certain stimuli (e.g. snakes and spiders in the case of Specific Phobia) and panic attacks that occur 'out of the blue'. Tom was able to understand that in Panic Disorder, individuals fear the consequences of the panic attack rather than exposure to a specific object or situation.

Using supervision to improve procedural knowledge and skill

Simply reading about or being told how to do something does not help the trainee to convert this into 'procedural knowledge and skill'. In terms of supporting procedural skills, supervisors can provide supervisees with more opportunities for role-play, both in terms of frequency and duration.

Sonny understood the rationale for undertaking reliving in the treatment of PTSD, however, he was unsure how long this should take, how many hot-spots to focus on and how to check that the client was accessing the memory effectively. Sonny was at the 'Knows how' stage but needed support to get to 'shows how'. His supervisor, Sonia, modelled this for him by asking Sonny to role-play a current client whilst she 'walked him through' the experience of reliving.

Supervisor tip

A method known as Deliberate Practice (covered in more detail in Chapter 15) is especially well suited to supervision, whereby supervisees practice a skill several times in a row, adjusting their style each time, based on live feedback (Vaz et al., 2025).

Basma had previously worked within an Eating Disorders Service and had developed considerable confidence and competence using CBT approaches for treating problems such as Anorexia or Bulimia. Despite possessing the declarative knowledge, Basma felt unsure of how to deliver some of the anxiety disorder protocols. Basma had taken up a new post in a Primary Care service and was expected to treat clients with Panic Disorder which she had no experience working with. Basma 'shadowed' some of Ramesh's therapy sessions to increase her procedural knowledge and used Deliberate Practice in supervision to try out methods that she was less familiar with using such as worry exposure.

Interpersonal skills

In terms of interpersonal skills, the trainee often draws upon their 'personal self' (e.g. who they are outside of being a therapist) to display empathy and validation with their clients. Understandably, individuals will vary considerably in their 'baseline' interpersonal skills. For example, some people are naturally more attuned to the feelings of others and those who are coming into CBT having worked as a counsellor might have already 'sharpened' their skills in this area. Having lived experience of mental health difficulties or experience of accessing personal therapy gives a perspective 'from the client's chair' which could also help in this skill domain (Limper-Menapace, 2025).

The role of self-practice and self-reflection

The reflective system is the part that helps therapists to compare theory with what they have learned in clinical practice, thereby fine-tuning their skills and understanding of a problem from different angles. Novice CBT practitioners may have a tendency to hold fairly rigid rules about when to use a particular formulation or technique therefore, reflective strategies such as applying CBT methods to one's own life (known as Self-Practice/Self-Reflection; SP/SR; Bennett-Levy et al., 2001) can help them to develop a more sophisticated understanding of the approach.

Applying CBT methods to one's own difficulties via informal self-practice or more formally as SP/SR can help to enhance empathy for clients. SP/SR has been shown to create an emotional bridge between the personal and the emerging 'therapist self' (Bennett-Levy & Finlay-Jones, 2018) and will be covered in more detail later in the book. For example, applying CBT methods to their own negative thoughts, difficult emotions and urges to avoid difficult situations can shift therapists from having an intellectual understanding of a topic or technique to a more *heart* level grasp of it.

> Trudie struggled to understand why many of her clients were unable to generate alternative thoughts when using a thought record. Her supervisor, Sonia, suggested that they both try to restructure one of their own frequently occurring Negative Automatic Thoughts within the supervision session. Trudie recognised that even as a therapist, this task was difficult for her and reflected that she had newfound empathy and compassion for her clients when asked to undertake this exercise.

What makes a highly effective therapist?

The ultimate aim of helping to build conceptual, technical and interpersonal skills within supervision is to produce highly effective therapists, but what sets apart those that achieve the best outcomes from the rest? In simple terms, highly effective therapists are those that tend to achieve better results for their clients.

Bennett-Levy (2019) summarises the research related to characteristics of highly effective therapists, showing that strong interpersonal (IP) skills consistently feature in the top performers. This might be somewhat surprising for CBT practitioners given that so much emphasis is placed upon adherence to and competence in, the delivery of specific formulations and interventions for different disorders (e.g. Roth & Pilling, 2007). Given the homogeneity of most CBT training courses (e.g. BABCP, 2025), what leads to some therapists having better IP skills than others, and is this something that can be cultivated within supervision?

How trainable are interpersonal skills?

Before answering this question, it is important to consider what is meant by 'interpersonal skills'. Bennett-Levy (2019) identifies self-awareness, interpersonal beliefs/attitudes and reflective skills as being key elements in this regard.

Self-awareness

This micro-skill might help us to reflect upon our own conscious and unconscious biases, accept our role in any ruptures that might occur in therapy or supervision and to acknowledge when we over-identify with certain clients (e.g. when she shared certain beliefs or life experiences as them). It can also help us to detect early signs of burnout in ourselves such as compassion fatigue and emotional exhaustion (McLean et al., 2003). Reviewing video recordings in supervision is one means of increasing self-awareness. Viewing ourselves from this perspective (once we get past the self-consciousness) has the potential to help us work on improving our attunement to the client (e.g. by observing our body language and displays of empathy within a given session). Personal Practices such as mindfulness can also help us to become a 'watcher' of our thoughts, emotions and urges (Bennett-Levy & Finlay-Jones, 2018). At times, judicious use of self-disclosure can aid the course of therapy and high self-awareness helps the individual to reflect upon the function and appropriateness of a self-disclosure (Henretty & Levitt, 2010).

Interpersonal beliefs

Also referred to at times as our 'interpersonal schemas' (Moorey & Lavender, 2019), these cognitive structures are likely to be formed earlier in life, before our therapy training and are linked to such matters as how easy we find it to trust other people. Certain 'rules for living' govern our interactions with others, influencing what we 'should' or 'should not' say or do. Without sufficient awareness of this, mistrust schemas can interfere with therapist relationships with their clients and supervisors. Leahy (2002) discusses the significance of 'emotional schemas' whereby individuals hold maladaptive beliefs (e.g. 'I can't cope with this feeling'; 'others think I am weak') about the implications of experiencing certain emotions (e.g. anxiety). It is likely that emotional schemas are linked to interpersonal schemas, therefore conversations about their overlap might be useful within supervision. If therapists hold similar beliefs to their clients, this can lead to reluctance in asking them to face the most challenging but necessary parts of therapy (e.g. sitting with high levels of affect during exposure or behavioural experiments; Presley et al., 2023).

> There was the risk that Tom's history of experiencing Social Anxiety Disorder (SAD) and the fact that he viewed aspects of the CBT treatment for SAD aversive, could lead to avoiding certain aspects of this treatment with his clients. Ramesh could work with Tom to enhance his self-awareness around the ways in which he might respond differently to SAD cases.

The degree to which interpersonal and emotional schemas are addressed in CBT training is unknown, however the focus has generally been on the acquisition of technical rather than interpersonal or intrapersonal skills (Leahy, 2008). Personal therapy can help to address the impact of these schemas; however, this is not mandated in CBT training, certainly within the UK. As previously mentioned, SP/SR can help with both self-awareness and modifying therapist beliefs. Leahy (2001) also identified a range of therapist schemas that can be captured using a questionnaire and targeted within supervision.

Reflective skills

The DPR model views reflection as the 'engine' of lifelong learning with clinical or personal life experiences providing opportunities to reflect upon the storehouse of knowledge that we are accruing in relation to CBT theories and how to apply with different clients and populations (Bennett-Levy, 2006). In broad terms, we tend to either *reflect on action* (e.g. watching ourselves on video within supervision) or *reflect in action* (e.g. noticing yourself withdrawing from a client who talks incessantly and won't let you get a word in edgeways). When learning a new skill, one is often so focused on 'getting it right' that attention is biased, and certain things get missed. Reviewing recordings of therapy sessions helps with reflecting on what was missed and why. Supervisors can use a range of questions to promote self-reflection within their supervisees (James et al., 2008) and using tools such as Padesky's Supervision Consultation Worksheet (available from padesky.com) can help a therapist to reflect upon matters such as the quality of their case conceptualisation or strength of their therapeutic alliance.

> Tom can use his own experiences of Social Anxiety to 'track' instances where he might struggle to believe the effectiveness of certain CBT interventions for clients who also experience this problem. By modelling attention training in supervision, Ramesh was able to help Tom to feel more confident using it in his own life and seeing how this could be beneficial for his clients.

Understanding the 'heart' of CBT often involves experiences that deepen ones appreciation for the nuanced way that formulations are developed and for the pace in which different interventions are introduced within a course of treatment. Understanding our own core beliefs, rules and assumptions, maladaptive behaviours and maintaining cycles can help us to develop a more idiosyncratic approach to therapy and to anticipate aspects of this work that might generate difficult thoughts and feelings within us.

> Due to his past experiences of racism, Sonny became more aware of his stronger counter-transference reactions with clients who hold racist views. Sonia suggested that he draw out his own longitudinal formulation within supervision to help make sense of his triggers. In doing so, he also began to recognise how he might find himself 'over-identifying' with a client that has also experienced racism.

Reflecting in action is a more difficult skill to harness as it involves mindful awareness, self-awareness of our schemas, our triggers for over or under-identifying with certain clients and the emotional regulation skills that stop us from acting on behaviours that might lead to an impasse or rupture (Katzow & Safran, 2010). Anecdotal experience of supervising qualified CBT therapists would suggest that these skills do not automatically improve with the passage of time. Recognising one's own limitations as a therapist can be difficult and is often hampered by our personal schemas and our schemas about CBT. The good news is that reflective skills can also be sharpened through the range methods outlined in this book.

Questions for meta-supervision

My supervisee over-estimates their interpersonal skills, what is the most sensitive way of raising this with them?

My supervisee is struggling to put theory into practice, what are the best methods to support them?

Chapter summary

- The DPR model illustrates how therapist skills develop over time and how supervisors can support this process.
- Active methods such as role-play, modelling and SP/SR can support conceptual, technical and interpersonal development.
- Strong interpersonal skills (e.g. empathy, attunement, validation) are critical for becoming a highly effective therapist.
- It might be necessary for supervisors to encourage their supervisee to address personal schemas and emotional responses that may affect therapy delivery.

Recommended reading

Bennett-Levy, J. (2006). Therapist skills: A cognitive model of their acquisition and refinement. *Behavioural and Cognitive Psychotherapy*, 34, 57–78.

Chapter 6

Stages of therapist skill development

Introduction

The previous chapter gave an overview of the types of skills that supervision can help therapists in harnessing (e.g. theoretical knowledge, practical skills and reflective capacity), yet it is important to consider the speed at which these develop, and what this might look like at different stages of one's career. This chapter will introduce the Integrative Developmental Model (IDM; Stoltenberg & McNeill, 2010) as a framework for understanding certain stages that all therapists go through in their journey from novice to expert practitioner. The IDM is also useful for helping supervisors to anticipate common difficulties that are likely to be seen at each stage and which may have an impact on the supervisory relationship. It will also consider ways in which supervisors can adjust their style and methods to suit the development stage of each supervisee. Whilst the original four stages of the IDM have been retained, the system for monitoring skill development has been modified to make it more applicable to CBT therapists.

Growing pains

The challenges of being a complete novice in CBT are usually very apparent, with understandable anxiety about getting things wrong, looking incompetent, feeling stuck and being extremely reliant on the advice of supervisors and tutors. The self-criticism, the avoidance and the reassurance seeking are usually very easy for supervisors to spot. Indeed, the archetypal challenges of the CBT training experience are summarised in the spoof journal paper on 'Cognitive Therapy Training Stress Disorder' (Worthless et al., 2002).

In this instance, it is often very clear what the supervisor needs to do with trainees at these early stages of their development. For supervisees who are in the second half of their training, arrive at CBT training with some pre-existing knowledge and skills, or that are newly qualified, it can be more difficult to gauge what their needs are. This stage of development is often characterised by having some declarative knowledge but possibly, a rigid understanding of theory and how to apply it to clients whose problems look nothing like the ones in textbooks. This group of therapists often possess growing confidence (sometimes over-confidence) in using

DOI: 10.4324/9781003590620-7

certain interventions but might fail to grasp the nuances of when to use them and when not to (the 'when . . . then rules' that Bennett-Levy (2006) speaks of).

This presents a different challenge for supervisors as the over-reliance on getting 'the answers' that is seen in complete novices can be replaced by a rejection of the supervisors advice and feedback. This rejection can be overt (e.g. arguing with the supervisor or trying to engage in a debate) or covert (e.g. nodding politely and agreeing but then doing something completely different when they see the client). In these instances, it is useful to have a framework that helps both supervisors and supervisees to make sense of where they are in their development and what 'growing pains' to expect at different points.

The Integrative Developmental Model (IDM)

Fortunately, such a framework does exist, yet it might be unfamiliar to many CBT therapists, as it was to me, until a couple of years ago. Stoltenberg (1981) developed the IDM, a useful transtheoretical framework that helps us to understand recognisable stages of therapist development. In a nutshell, the IDM proposes that therapists move through four stages of skill development (Level 1, Level 2, Level 3 and Level 3 integrated). The final stage (3i) represents the attainment of 'master therapist' status and is not a destination that all therapists will get to for one reason or another (Skovholt & Jennings, 2017). The IDM also considers three cognitive structures that are consistent across these levels – *self and other awareness*; *motivation* and *autonomy* (see Figure 6.1)

As Figure 6.1 shows, the majority of trainee therapists will start at the bottom (Level 1), gradually moving their way up to the top. An exception to this might

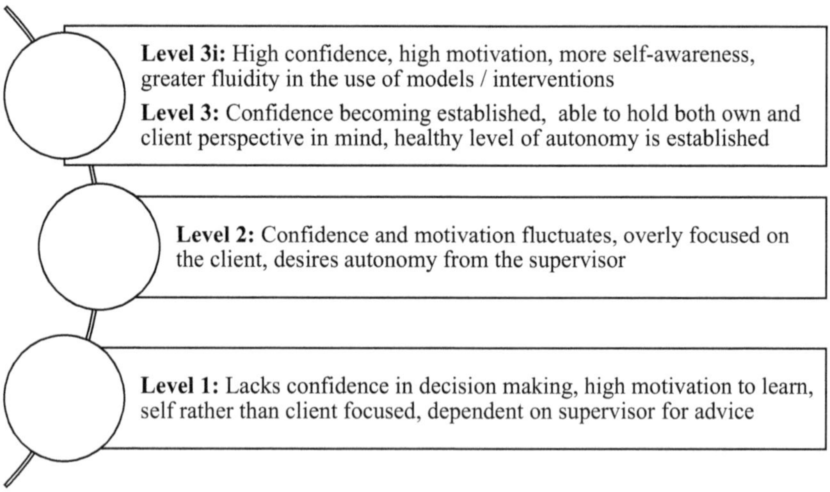

Figure 6.1 Characteristics of IDM Stages based on Stoltenberg and McNeill (2010).

be clinical psychologists who core training includes a significant CBT component who then attend 'top up' training post qualification (see Daley et al., 2022).

Using the IDM to guide supervision methods

Each stage of the IDM has certain 'hallmarks' associated with it and an awareness of these can be helpful for trainers and supervisors when considering the 'zone of proximal development' that each therapist is in at any given time, during training or post-qualification (Vygotsky, 1978).

Estimating where a supervisee is currently at in their development can help supervisors to select supervision methods that are most likely to help and can also assist supervisees in preparing appropriate supervision questions. For example, Level 1 therapists are likely to have quite basic questions about CBT theory and often require more supervisor modelling of formulations and interventions than qualified therapists (Gordon, 2012). Later stage trainees or qualified therapists who are moving towards Level 2, might bring different types of questions to supervision, questions that may be imbued with a deeper understanding of CBT theory and interventions. This might be in relation to working with more complex presentations or interpersonal difficulties such as experiencing strong emotions (e.g. counter-transference reactions) towards certain clients (Moorey & Lavender, 2019).

It is important to note that the length of time one has been delivering CBT does not equate to the IDM stage. For example, a therapist might stay in Stage 1 for longer than another who commenced their training at the same time. However, Stoltenberg and McNeill (2010) also talk about 'pseudo Level 3' therapists who can 'talk a good game' yet their clinical (procedural skills) do not reflect this.

Challenges in estimating the supervisees current stage of development

Whilst it is common practice to estimate the supervisees overall IDM Level, it is more likely that individuals will be at different levels in different skill domains. For example, the IDM recognises that individuals can be at different levels for different types of skills or clinical presentations. Therefore, a therapist who has worked with a high volume of depressed clients might be at Level 3 in that domain yet still be at Level 1 or 2 with certain anxiety disorders. Similarly, the pressure to acquire technical skills such as a range of formulations and interventions can mean that generic therapy skills such as empathic attunement often 'take a back seat' until the former are in place.

Reflective exercise

Are you already familiar with the IDM? If so, do you use it to inform your supervisory focus with different supervisees?

Using the IDM stages to select the most suitable supervisory methods

The IDM can guide supervisors to support therapists in several of these skill domains which are likely to consist of both declarative knowledge and procedural skill (Bennett-Levy, 2006). Figure 6.2 provides a visual representation of each skill that might be targeted within supervision, at any given time. With early-stage trainees there is often a more even 'split' because there is so much to learn. With later stage trainees, or qualified supervisees, a larger 'slice' of the pie chart will be devoted to agreed areas for development.

The domain headings are explained below but have been amended to make them more specific to the assessment of CBT related skill development.

CBT assessment skills

The professional requirements to train in CBT mean that trainees are usually highly skilled in undertaking generic mental health assessments (e.g. to establish suitability for accessing a service or to determine levels of risk). This domain refers to being able to conduct an assessment through a cognitive-behavioural lens, which at a basic level, involves eliciting information related to activating events and subsequent

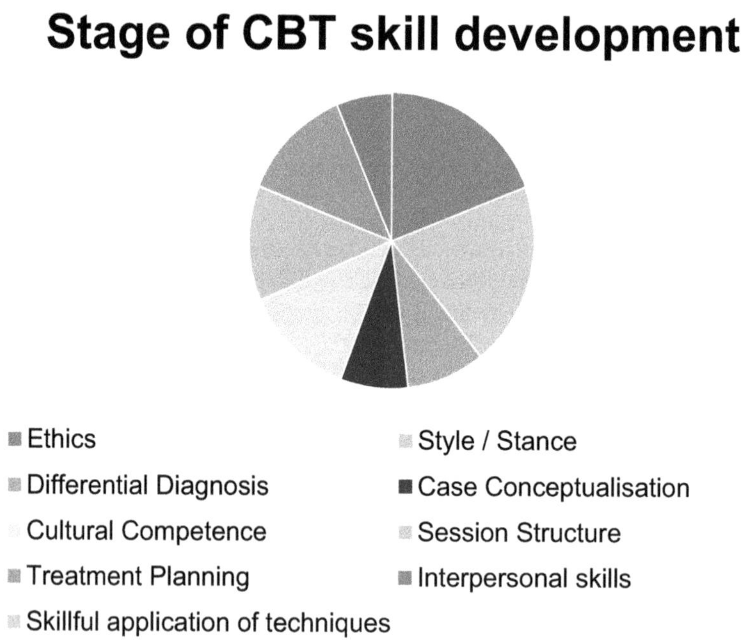

Figure 6.2 A pie chart of supervisory focus for early-stage trainees.

thoughts, emotions, bodily sensations and behavioural responses. At a more sophisticated level, this would be evidenced by the ability to identify rules, assumptions and core beliefs about self, others, world and the future (Beck et al., 1979, pa).

Case conceptualisation skills

Those new to CBT are often introduced to generic five areas diagrams (e.g. Padesky & Mooney, 1990) before moving on to the disorder-specific models. More advanced skills in this domain might be evidenced by adapting these models to take account of intersectionality (Crenshaw, 1989) or using transdiagnostic formulations where client problems do not fit neatly within a specific model (e.g. 'the mental crusher'; Butler et al., 2010).

Session structure

The structure of CBT can differ significantly from that to which many mental health professionals have been accustomed to working prior to entering training (e.g. Wilcockson, 2020). Agenda setting and homework review are key indicators of emerging skills, however, retaining a focus on the agreed problem areas and goals can be a challenge for both new and experienced therapists alike.

Skilful application of techniques

This skill domain includes knowledge of a range of interventions (e.g. behavioural experiments), their intended use and the typical sequence in which they are used during a course of treatment. As one becomes more experienced, therapists develop 'when . . . then' rules which help them to consider how to use interventions more flexibly (e.g. in relation to treatment obstacles; Bennett-Levy, 2019).

Treatment planning

The IDM also suggests that we might expect to observe differences in how Level 1, 2 and 3 supervisees plan courses of treatment. For example, Level 1 supervisees might display extreme rigidity in the order in which they use interventions and the rules they have about which problem to start with when dealing with co-morbidity. Level 2 might be characterised by an overidentification with clients and colluding with their scepticism about the effectiveness of CBT. Finally, Level 3 supervisees might display meta-competences characterised by flexibility with fidelity to the overarching cognitive model (Kendall & Frank, 2018).

Interpersonal skills

It is often said within CBT that a good therapeutic alliance is necessary, but insufficient on its own to bring about change and therefore symptom reduction. Nevertheless, interpersonal effectiveness is an item on the widely used Cognitive Therapy Scale Revised (CTS-R; Blackburn et al., 2001) and therefore, trainees must learn to strike the balance between validation, empathy, compassion and sticking with the structure of CBT (Wade & Waller, 2025). For example, some therapists place too much importance on trying to soothe or validate the client at the expense of pushing for change, meaning that this can compromise the effectiveness of the treatment and delay skill development in other domains (Waller, 2009).

Cultural competence

Supervisors are encouraged to explore any conscious or unconscious biases that their supervisees might have, which could in turn, negatively impact on their clinical work. Whilst cultural competence is not a destination, we can look for signs of how well the supervisees considers factors such as intersectionality and social GRRRAAACCEEESSS (Burnham, 2012) within their formulations, supervision questions and interventions.

Understanding of ethics

Awareness of ethics with CBT treatment might begin more generic topics (e.g. safeguarding) or tasks that were a core part of their previous professional roles (e.g. ethical practice as a nurse). Higher IDM stages are likely to be characterised by an increasingly sophisticated understanding of the types of ethical dilemmas that might emerge (e.g. when and when not to use self-disclosure).

Style and stance

This category does not feature within the original IDM domains, however it is added here due to the potential fundamental value of checking in with how well 'aligned' the supervisee is with CBT overall (Roscoe & Wilbraham, 2024). Some will begin their training being highly aligned with CBT, characterised by positive attitudes towards theory and interventions (Wolff & Auckenthaler, 2014). This might change during training (e.g. finding suitable training cases) or when they move to IDM level 2. Conversely, others will be less aligned at the start of training, yet once certain misconceptions about CBT have been addressed, and they have experienced it working in clinical practice, their alignment might improve.

Supervisor tip

You might wish to administer the Alignment to CBT Scale (see Appendix 5) if you suspect a weak or weakening alignment. Whilst there is no cut off score to indicate the optimal alignment, a lower overall score or a low score on specific items might warrant further discussion.

Anticipating challenges within the IDM stages of development

Some Level 1 therapists will be extremely anxious about making mistakes and seek excessive reassurance from their supervisors, which can be frustrating for supervisors who value independence in their supervisees. Conversely, some Level 2 therapists will display over-confidence at times whilst returning to feeling helpless or disillusioned with the model at others. This later situation can manifest as reluctance or refusal to accept the supervisor's recommendations and ultimately creates the conditions for a rupture to ensue. Chapters 18 and 19 provides some ideas for how to manage these challenges to the supervisory relationship.

The focus up to this point has been the value of the IDM to supervisors, however, an awareness of the IDM can help supervisees to manage any unrealistic expectations they might hold about what they 'should' know or be able to achieve at different points in their development. This is especially useful for those prone to perfectionism, such as Tom (Presley, 2025).

> Tom had always been a high achiever throughout school, college and undergraduate studies and he had 'sailed through' his Psychological Wellbeing Practitioner (PWP) training and was surprised about how difficult he was finding CBT training. He frequently expressed frustration with himself in supervision, indicating to Ramesh that he held very demanding standards for himself.

For qualified therapists, they can also feel the pressure to demonstrate competence with every clinical problem (e.g. 'I'm qualified so I should know what I am doing'). This was the case with Basma who was very confident in using CBT for Eating Disorders but less familiar with CBT for common mental health problems.

> Basma had enjoyed using the Fairburn (2008) CBT-E protocol due to it following clear stages of treatment, however, she felt unsure where to start when treating clients with anxiety disorders. Basma also struggled to see how many of the interventions that she used previously are transdiagnostic and could underpin her work with her new clients (e.g. self-monitoring). Basma became annoyed with herself saying in supervision that 'she should be able to do this by now'.

Supervisor tip: watch out for supervisor perfectionism!

The IDM has also been applied to supervisor development and many supervisors, especially those at Level 1 of the IDM, feel a huge amount of pressure to 'get it right' in supporting their supervisees. This can lead to beliefs such as 'I must have all the answers' and 'I should never make mistakes'. 'Fusing' with these thoughts can lead to anxiety and shame which some supervisors will then manage through avoidance (e.g. choosing not to model interventions in case the supervisee criticises them). This can result in them 'telling' supervisees what to do rather than 'showing' them.

Ramesh explained the IDM stages to Basma and together they had a go at mapping out where she might be in terms of her skill development across different domains. Ramesh used the 'IDM Snapshot' form to generate a score for each domain (see Table 6.1). This helped Basma to recognise her many strengths and to also be more compassionate towards herself.

Table 6.1 IDM snapshot for supervisees (adapted to fit specifically with CBT)

Supervisee Initials	*B.A.*
Frequency of Supervision	Monthly
Level of CBT Training/Status	Post Graduate Diploma (Qualified)
Length of time qualified	1 year
Approximate Overall IDM Level	2
Specific IDM Skill Domains Ratings (1, 2, 3 or 3i)	
Assessment Skills	3
Case Conceptualisation Skills	2
Session Structure	3
Skilful application of techniques (e.g. CBT Interventions)	2
Treatment Planning	2
Interpersonal Skills	2
Cultural Competence	3
Understanding of Ethics	3
Style/Stance (Alignment to CBT)	3

Questions for meta-supervision

My supervisee is very dependent on me to tell them what to do with every clinical decision. How should I manage this?

It seems as if my supervisee is paying lip service to the suggestions I make in supervision. I'm concerned that they see coming here as a tick box exercise. What should I do?

Chapter summary

- The IDM is a useful framework for supervisors and supervisees to anticipate common challenges both in therapy and within the supervisory relationship.
- Knowledge of these structures and levels of the IDM can normalise some of the struggles that novice therapists face and can help supervisors to tailor their approach accordingly.
- The IDM can help with developing goals for supervision or help to indicate the supervision methods that are likely to be most suitable for promoting learning.
- An understanding of the IDM levels can guide supervisors towards using the most effective interventions at each stage of therapist skill development.
- The 'IDM Snapshot' form can be used to capture a summary of each supervisee's IDM profile (see Table 6.1).

Recommended reading

Stoltenberg, C. (1981). Approaching supervision from a developmental perspective: The counselor complexity model. *Journal of counseling Psychology*, 28(1), 59.

Chapter 7

Identifying blocks to therapist skill development

Introduction

This chapter covers a range of potential obstacles or 'roadblocks' that supervisors face when trying to support therapists in developing or enhancing their CBT skills. Holding in mind the Integrative Developmental Model (IDM; Stoltenberg, 1981) in the previous chapter, it would be naive to assume that this only happens with trainee therapists, therefore supervisors should also hold in mind qualified supervisees when reading this chapter.

The Declarative Procedural Reflective (DPR) model (Bennett-Levy, 2006) that was summarised in Chapter 5 helps to guide supervisors towards targeting various skill domains such as declarative knowledge (e.g. understanding the various theories that underpin CBT), procedural skill (e.g. being able to demonstrate competence in the use of different interventions) and the capacity for self-reflection (e.g. to recognise how one's beliefs impact how one delivers CBT). There are two key aspects to this model that can help us to anticipate where some supervisees will get 'stuck' during their clinical work. First, the three domains of knowledge and skill (declarative, procedural and reflective) provide supervisors with tangible avenues to explore and track across supervision sessions. Second, the DPR model hypothesises the presence of two 'selves' that contribute towards therapist skill development. There is an emerging 'therapist self', borne out of the 'input' from lectures, reading, clinical interactions and supervision. There is also contribution from the 'personal self', which contains all of their pre-therapy training beliefs and experiences. Understanding how these multiple selves influence one another can help supervisors to anticipate and overcome common barriers.

Common 'roadblocks' to explore within supervision

In addition to knowing the skill domains in which supervisees might struggle and, need additional support, it is useful to understand why they might get stuck. For example, whilst the IDM model describes the stages that all therapists pass through, we need to understand why some take longer to move from Level 1 to 2 or from 2 to 3. A series of 'roadblocks' are outlined below, and supervisors can map these out with a supervisee, or do this as an exercise within meta-supervision.

DOI: 10.4324/9781003590620-8

Roadblock 1: Insufficient declarative knowledge

From a contextual perspective, factors such as the quality of teaching during one's period of training, level of engagement with literature (e.g. reading and comprehending key journal papers or books), the suitability of initial clients and being able to 'shadow' more experienced peers, all contribute towards the development of declarative knowledge. Whilst much of this is outside of the supervisor's direct control, it is essential to build mechanisms within supervision to gauge declarative knowledge.

> Basma brought a recording to supervision where she had been working with a client whose primary problem was Generalised Anxiety Disorder. When playing the recording, Ramesh noticed that Basma had used cognitive restructuring (CR) on a specific worry. At the end of the video clip, Ramesh explored Basma's rationale for using CR and asked how this fitted with her understanding of the Dugas protocol.
>
> (see Robichaud et al., 2019)

Roadblock 2: Deficits in procedural skill

Knowing what to do and being able to do it competently are two different things, therefore supervisors need to check that the supervisee can 'show how' in addition to 'knowing how' (Miller, 1990).

> Tom felt confident using low intensity interventions to treat Depression such as activity scheduling and thought challenging. Unfortunately, despite attending the relevant teaching, Tom continued to use activity scheduling in the same way that he did when he was a Psychological Wellbeing Practitioner (PWP). It seemed that Tom was not grasping the difference between high and low intensity in relation to activity scheduling and behavioural activation.

For Tom, there is the possibility of him being 'unconsciously incompetent' in the use of CBT methods. Behavioural activation (BA) as taught and delivered in a low intensity format is quite different from the high intensity version (Roth & Pilling, 2007) yet experience suggests that trainees from a PWP background often underestimate these differences.

The principles of schema development and maintenance can help us to make sense of why this occurs. For example, Tom is likely to assimilate new knowledge about BA into his existing mental representation (schema) of how to deliver this (Piaget, 1948). Supervisors need to create the conditions for supervisees to accommodate new schematic information.

> Ramesh decided to model the use of high intensity BA within supervision for Tom and asked him to consider what was similar and what was different to the low intensity version that he was familiar with. Ramesh then asked Tom to

role play introducing this to a client and afterwards they reflected on the main differences.

Don't assume competence in the absence of evidence!

Deficits in procedural skills are inevitable with those who are undertaking training, however some supervisees appear to struggle more than others. Observing the supervisees work through reviewing recording of therapy sessions or undertaking skills rehearsal provides the best way of checking in on this. These are fairly common practices during training, yet research and anecdotal experience suggest that supervisors mainly rely on what qualified therapists tell them happened in a therapy session rather than being able to observe it for themselves (Liness et al., 2017; Townend et al., 2002).

Supervisor tip

Whilst many supervisees will be acutely aware of their gaps in knowledge or skills, some supervisees may be unaware of their incompetence ('unconscious incompetence').

Roadblock 3: Use of safety behaviours

Some of the core skills in CBT are more challenging to master than others, such as guided discovery (Waltman et al., 2017). A study by Roscoe et al. (2022b) sought to understand the barriers to acquiring skills in this area. One of the most significant findings was that trainees often revert to using tried and tested ways of working with clients when they feel anxious or uncertain about the outcome of a Socratic Dialogue. For example, PWPs who are well accustomed to providing psychoeducation, may revert to telling the client what they need to do to feel better, rather than engaging in guided discovery. We can conceptualise this as a therapist 'safety behaviour' that is relieving their anxiety in the short term but ultimately preventing them from developing confidence and competence in certain skill domains. In this sense, supervisors need to be vigilant for the fact that supervisees might know what they should be doing, but their anxiety about their own or their client's distress is leading to them avoiding or minimising the use of certain CBT methods (Presley et al., 2023).

Roadblock 4: Problematic beliefs about CBT

It is not uncommon for trainees to hold a range of negative beliefs about CBT that lead to them rejecting certain aspects of the structure or avoiding specific interventions (Parker & Waller, 2017). One might ask why an individual chooses to train in CBT if it is so unacceptable to them? Research suggests that there are multiple motivations to training in CBT (e.g. to enhance one's career, for a higher salary, better shift patterns) so it is often not simply a case of trainees being those who are 'well aligned' with CBT (Roscoe & Wilbraham, 2024). Even when they are, some therapists fear upsetting or retraumatising their clients due to misconceptions about what happens during interventions such as reliving (see Murray et al., 2022).

> Sonny, a trainee clinical psychologist undertaking a CBT Pathway as part of his doctorate holds a range of negative beliefs about CBT. He has used aspects of CBT when he was an assistant psychologist but after his person-centred counsellor training he holds the view that CBT is a 'sticking plaster', failing to get to the 'root' of a person's problems.

This example shows how Sonny's 'Previous Professional Selves' (counsellor and assistant psychologist) have led to the construction of an overly negative schema about CBT. Sonny also has a competing 'Clinical Psychologist Self' whereby he is also learning about other modalities during his doctoral training. In comparison to those who are leaving behind another professional identity (e.g. PWPs), Sonny has to juggle the development of two therapist selves.

Roadblock 5: Relinquishing behaviours associated with previous professional roles

It is also fairly common for trainees to want to hold on to certain ways of working that were central to their previous roles. For example, social workers will have certain ways of interacting with clients that differ from how Occupational Therapists would work (Wilcockson, 2020).

> Trudie initially worked as a mental health social worker within the same CAMHS team and self-funded to train in CBT where there was a considerable emphasis on the 'third wave'. During her training, Trudie held dual roles, continuing to be a care co-ordinator and case manager for several young people whilst managing a separate 'CBT caseload'.

In this example, Trudie has experienced difficulties in being able to relinquish her previous professional role entirely due to ongoing care co-ordination requirements within the workplace. Trudie is trying to establish her CBT therapist Self; however, she is still required to act in the role of social worker on occasions. Another potential challenge for supervision is around what Trudie constitutes as 'CBT'. Having been exposed to a significant proportion of lectures on third wave approaches such as mindfulness, Acceptance and Commitment Therapy and Dialectical Behaviour Therapy, Trudie's supervisor will have to assess her competence in using 'wave two' approaches given that she is employed to deliver these for the most part.

Roadblock 6: Epistemic style

During CBT training, theories are introduced about how mental health problems arise and how they are best managed, and these can be radically different from existing personal or professional beliefs. For example, some nurses might strongly believe that mental health problems such as depression arise from a biological cause (e.g. chemical imbalance that is best managed through medication) whilst counsellors might struggle to accept the more directive style and structure of CBT (Wilcockson, 2022). On a person level, some individuals might believe that exposing individuals to highly distressing situations or memories is unethical (Deacon et al., 2013). Epistemic style (ES) is a term that describes our 'worldview' which is often taken to be 'truth' and is rarely consciously questioned (Lee et al., 2013). ES could be largely influenced by life experiences prior to CBT training, or it could be shaped by professional experiences. For example, the decision to train and work as a nurse could be shaped by personal life experiences and being a nurse can shape personal 'self' beliefs.

Reflective exercise

Which of these roadblocks have you observed in any of your supervisees past or present?
How have you managed the impact of this?

Table 7.1 provides some examples of potential focal points during supervision which relate to common obstacles that arise in relation to skill acquisition. It considers how these might present differently amongst trainees and qualified practitioners.

Table 7.1 Common obstacles and focal points within supervision

Area of focus within supervision	*Obstacle to skill acquisition*	*Trainees*	*Qualified Practitioners*
Declarative knowledge of disorders, models and interventions	Misconceptions about theories, struggle to draw out model components, sequence of interventions	Focus of learning some skills takes the focus away from others	Did not get to work with some problems during training
Confidence and competence in applying differential	Struggling to spot the 'hallmarks' of disorders or missing out	Fitting clients to protocols	Rejection of protocols or diagnosis

(Continued)

Table 7.1 (Continued)

Area of focus within supervision	*Obstacle to skill acquisition*	*Trainees*	*Qualified Practitioners*
diagnosis, formulations and interventions in practice	important parts of an intervention		
Addressing negative beliefs or fears about aspects of CBT	Unwilling to use certain interventions due to concerns about outcome	Anxiety about 'getting it wrong'/ look incompetent	Continuing to avoid/reject certain aspects of treatment
Letting go of old ways of conceptualising/ working or 'making room for' CBT	Reverting to what is known or preferred when uncertain	Telling the client what to do	Badging third wave interventions as CBT
Justifying clinician decisions	Rationale for or sequence of interventions	Rigidity with treatment sequencing	Excessive relational focus

Questions for meta-supervision

How do I help my supervisees to identify problematic beliefs?
My supervisee seems to be struggling with role transition, what are the best ways to help them with this?

Chapter summary

- The DPR model helps supervisors to identify skill domains in which therapists may struggle.
- Anxiety about 'getting it wrong' or making clients worse can lead therapists to revert to familiar but less effective methods. This can hinder development of core CBT skills such as guided discovery.
- Previous professional identities (e.g. counsellor, assistant psychologist) as well as deeply held beliefs about mental health (e.g. biological vs psychological models) may foster negative schemas about CBT, whilst holding competing identities (e.g. clinical psychologist vs CBT therapist) can create an internal conflict for therapists.

Recommended reading

Wilcockson, M. D. (2020). Transition to cognitive behavioural therapy from different core professional backgrounds: Three grounded theory studies. *The Cognitive Behaviour Therapist*, 13, E35. https://doi.org/10.1017/S1754470X20000331

Chapter 8

Understanding supervisory drift

Introduction

The previous chapter considered supervisee specific factors that may interfere with skill development; here, attention is given to supervisor beliefs and behaviours that serve to (often inadvertently) undermine the core functions of supervision. In essence, supervisors who consistently fail to undertake core normative, formative or restorative tasks that are deemed necessary to support therapist skill development can be seen as 'drifting'. This chapter will highlight how certain beliefs, contextual pressures and cultural norms interact to perpetuate 'supervisory drift' (Pugh & Margetts, 2020; Roscoe, 2021b).

Defining supervisory drift

The term 'supervisory drift' (SD) has been used by various authors to describe supervisory practices that run the risk of becoming ineffective or, at worst, harmful (Milne, 2020). The tasks that we deem 'necessary' within supervision can be derived from transtheoretical features of supervision, such as those described in earlier chapters – namely, attending to normative, formative and restorative issues (Proctor, 1994) and modality-specific features, such as a focus on achieving and maintaining clinical competence and treatment fidelity.

How do we identify supervision practices that are deemed 'sub-standard' and that drift away from their intended purposes? Firstly, we need a clear and succinct definition, and this is offered by Pugh and Margetts (2020), who proposed that SD occurs when 'core components of supervision (e.g. outcomes monitoring, direct observation, mutual feedback) are omitted, avoided or deprioritised, resulting in a gap between supervisory theory and practice' (p. 5).

Prevalence of SD

Samples of supervisory practices appear to confirm that there is a gap between what supervisory theories suggest should happen and what actually takes place.

DOI: 10.4324/9781003590620-9

For example, a survey by Townend et al. (2002) found that 72% never bring videos to supervision and 94% never use role-play. More recently, Roscoe et al. (2022a) carried out semi-structured interviews with a sample of CBT supervisors and supervisees to understand how they use supervision and the factors that influence their decisions. The key findings from this study suggested:

- A lack of clarity around which, if any supervision model should guide supervision sessions
- The view that existing supervision models such as the Newcastle 'Cakestand' (Armstrong & Freeston, 2006) lack credibility or are seen as too complex to understand and implement
- That supervisors and supervisees held silent assumptions about each other's role within supervision (e.g. what they believed the other person 'should' be doing), and this led to feelings of frustration
- A pervasive fear of being exposed/judged negatively led to avoidance of showing videos (this was evident even amongst experienced CBT therapists who were supervisors themselves)

The indicators of drift proposed by Pugh and Margetts provide supervisors and meta-supervisors with examples of what to look for when considering if this is occurring. For example, the absence of outcome monitoring is likely to mean that the supervisor is largely taking the supervisee's word for the fact that their clients are making progress. Similarly, without direct observation (e.g. watching a video) it is also difficult to judge that the supervisee is practising competently, even if they are describing interventions that show fidelity to the model.

> Sonny rarely brought recordings of his clinical work to supervision sessions. When asked about this, he would either say that his clients were unwilling to be recorded or that there had been a tech issue that had prevented the recording from being useable. Most supervision sessions consisted of him asking questions about CBT theory or explaining why he didn't think CBT techniques would work for most of his clients. At times, Sonia would get drawn into debates about why CBT was suitable for his clients or would 'give up' asking to see evidence of Sonny's work to avoid straining the relationship. Without viewing how Sonny interacts with his clients, it is difficult for his supervisor to evaluate his procedural skills. Furthermore, the nature of Sonny's supervision questions led to debate or didactic instruction rather than modelling or role-play.

By failing to observe Sonny's clinical work, there is the potential for problems like therapist drift to ensue (Waller, 2009), hence the need to identify and minimise the occurrence of SD.

Supervisor tip

The intention here is not to demonise case discussion or shame supervisors if they are not using active methods regularly. The intention is to highlight why active methods are essential for helping supervisors to more accurately gauge therapist skill development.

An expanded definition

Whilst the Pugh and Margetts definition tells us what is missing from supervision when it drifts, it does not tell us the reasons for drift arising or the consequences of drift. For this reason, I have sought to expand this definition using Proctor's (1994) core functions and to consider the potential casual mechanisms and consequences of the gap between supervisory theory and practice.

I view SD as occurring when any of the three core functions of supervision (normative, formative or restorative) are consistently avoided, underemphasised, or discouraged within a supervisory relationship. This encapsulates all of the tasks that Pugh & Margetts describe but expands this to include the need to address restorative needs such as the supervisee's safety within the relationship and their mental wellbeing. The key word here is 'consistently', as it is likely that some degree of drift is normal and does not lead to an ineffective learning experience for the supervisee. Supervisors need to balance the roles of being judge, educator and listener, and this means that one of these 'hats' will take centre stage from time to time in response to the supervisee's agenda.

Understanding factors that drive SD

Why do supervision dyads frequently avoid or underuse the most powerful supervision methods? Looking at the wider supervision literature, SD is likely to arise because of supervisor and supervisee beliefs, how these beliefs interact and how they are reinforced within certain contexts.

> Basma and Ramesh both had a dislike for watching videos of themselves working with clients. Despite having done it during his own training, Ramesh still found it uncomfortable and assumed that Basma would find it extremely uncomfortable too. In addition to this, Basma had a high caseload and wanted to discuss several clients at each supervision session. Noticing her reluctance and the pressure to 'cram' all of these cases into one hour a month, Ramesh sought to ease her anxiety by not asking her to bring videos. This communicated to Basma that videos were both 'a big deal' and not essential components of supervision.

This example demonstrates how problematic beliefs and supervision-interfering behaviours (SIBS) may take the form of collusion between supervisor and supervisee to avoid mutually aversive tasks (see Milne et al., 2009). For others, there might be an ignorance on behalf of either party as to what they 'should' be doing. For example, it is not uncommon in NHS settings to start supervising before one has had any supervisor training, meaning that supervisors often draw upon their own experiences of supervision to guide their practice (Roscoe & Scullane, 2025). For supervisees, they might not know how to prepare effectively for CBT supervision (see Appendix 2) and therefore require 'socialising' to the structure (which might be very different to the types of supervision they have had in previous roles).

Lastly, SD could be the product of a rupture, whereby the supervisee no longer feels safe enough to share important information with their supervisor (see Mehr et al., 2010), or the supervisor has become so frustrated by the supervisee's avoidance that they stop asking them to bring recordings to supervision, as was the case with Sonia and Sonny.

Addressing wider influences on the practice of supervision

The research that I have undertaken with CBT supervisors and supervisees, combined with my own experiences of delivering supervision and supervisor training, suggest that these beliefs are also influenced by cultural and contextual factors (see Figure 8.1). I refer to these factors as the '3 C's, which relate to the *cognitions* of the supervisor and supervisee, the *context* in which supervision and therapy is undertaken (e.g. NHS versus private practice) and the influence of *culture* (e.g. norms around supervision practices and cultural norms specific to the supervisee). It is hypothesised that these factors may interact to weaken the overall quality of supervision, resulting in supervisory drift (Pugh & Margetts, 2020; Roscoe, 2021b).

Cognitions

Beliefs about how supervision should be, based on earlier experiences

Schema theory suggests that we form mental templates of different situations, expecting these patterns to be repeated in future interactions (Segal, 1988). Supervision is no exception; therefore, prior experiences of supervision are likely to be the biggest driver of what supervisees believe supervision to be about. This extends to beliefs about what the supervisor will or will not do or say and what their role and responsibilities are as supervisees. Those who have felt unsafe in previous supervisory relationships might naturally try to avoid experiencing conflict or abuse, and this might result in behaviours that serve to reduce feelings of anxiety or shame.

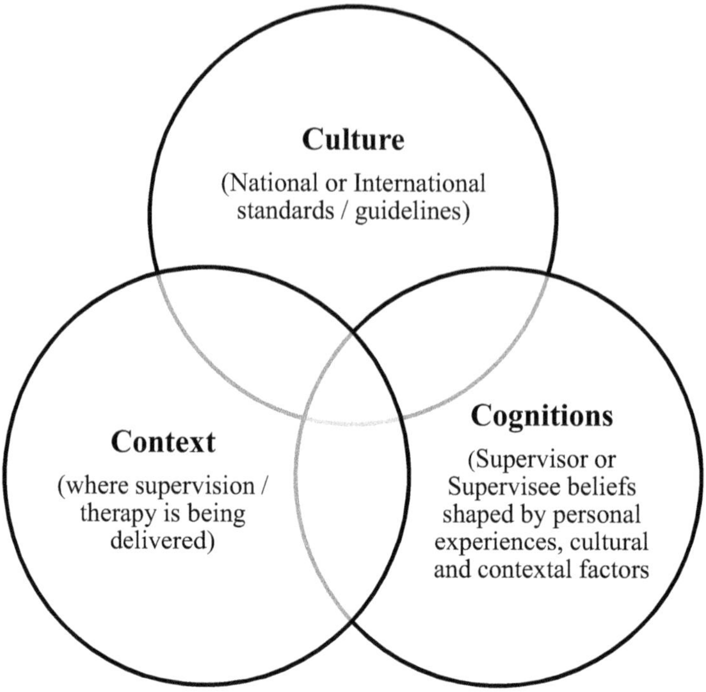

Figure 8.1 The 3 C's of supervision.

Personal characteristics

As previous chapters have shown, personal characteristics of the supervisor or supervisee will influence how they think and behave within therapeutic and supervisory relationships. For example, Simpson-Southward et al. (2018) found that psychological factors such as Intolerance of Uncertainty (IU) and low self-esteem (LSE) were associated with a greater potential for supervisory drift. A supervisor who is high on IU might worry about the outcome of an active method and 'play it safe' by sticking to case discussion. Similarly, therapist schemas such as 'need for approval' (Leahy, 2001) may lead to the supervisor placing the emotional needs of the supervisee above their need to assess competence, adherence and ethical practice.

Context

Context refers to the environment in which supervision takes place, whether that be NHS, university or PP. An important contextual factor relates to the time that is available for preparation before supervision sessions. For example, if no time is given to prepare for supervision within a specific service, then this can impact the quality of supervision questions that are formulated. The format of supervision (e.g. whether it is online or face to face) might also be influenced by the context, with peer supervision being more common than one-to-one due to staffing levels. Dual relationships (e.g. where the supervisor is also one's line manager) can present difficulties in the supervisee feeling safe enough to express concerns about their caseload or working conditions.

Culture

In terms of culture, we can think of there being 'macro' and 'micro' level cultural attitudes that affect supervision. For example, the micro-culture is what goes on within a specific organisation (e.g. an NHS Trust or team within a Trust) and is therefore shaped by the context (e.g. service pressures). The macro-culture relates to the messages that are given to supervisors and supervisees from larger organisations such as accrediting bodies (e.g. BABCP). Cultural norms about what we do or do not do in supervision (e.g. Roscoe, 2020a) influence the cognitions (beliefs) that supervisors and supervisees hold about the importance of various supervisory tasks. For example, there is a cultural norm that CBT therapists must be accredited as practitioners across most NHS services, yet there is no expectation that one should hold supervisor accreditation. Unless one is an accredited supervisor, there is no obligation to attend ongoing CPD for supervisory skills, thus giving the message that enhancing one's skills as a supervisor is not essential.

Reflective exercise

Considering the 3 C's, do any of these factors have an impact on the content and style of your supervision sessions?

What might the consequences be for your supervisees?

Putting it all together, supervisees like Basma, Sonny, Tom and Trudie, who work in time-pressured services (context), might struggle to carve out the space to review video clips in advance of supervision or to think in detail about what they wish to use the supervision session for. Their beliefs (cognitions) about the purpose and scope of supervision (e.g. 'letting off steam', getting advice) might clash with those of their supervisor, or their beliefs might be reinforced by the supervisor (knowingly or unknowingly), communicating the idea that active methods are not important. Wider cultural attitudes towards supervision mean that their supervisors do not feel compelled to invest in 'topping up' their supervisory skills in the same way that they must with their therapy skills in order to maintain their accreditation.

Reducing the likelihood of SD

There are several 'safeguards' that supervisors can put in place to reduce the risk of SD. Firstly, regularly reviewing their use of active methods using the checklist in Chapter 2 is one way of reflecting on their practice. The second safeguard is to make sure that one accesses meta-supervision on a regular basis. Often, as is the case with our clinical work, we can struggle to 'helicopter up' to see our blind spots and biases; therefore, taking recordings of our supervision sessions to another supervisor can pay dividends in this respect. Finally, seeking feedback from our supervisees on their experiences of supervision with us can help to identify strengths and weaknesses which we can work on in meta-supervision or through attending further training.

Questions for meta-supervision

I have got out of the habit of asking supervisees to bring recordings to sessions. How do I reintroduce this without it seeming as if I think they are incompetent?

I'm not sure what my strengths and weaknesses are as a supervisor. Where do I start in terms of assessing this?

Chapter summary

- Supervisory Drift (SD) refers to supervision practices that omit or deprioritise essential components such as outcome monitoring, direct observation and mutual feedback. These omissions can undermine therapist development and compromise treatment fidelity.
- Normative, formative and restorative functions must be consistently addressed. Drift occurs when these are avoided or underemphasised.
- Verbal case discussion dominates CBT supervision, while active methods (e.g. role-play, video review) are underused, limiting accurate assessment of therapist skills.
- Supervisory drift often stems from shared avoidance, discomfort with active methods, or lack of training. Supervisors may replicate their own supervision experiences, and supervisees may not be adequately socialised into CBT supervision structures.

Recommended reading

Roscoe, J. (2021b). Conceptualising and managing supervisory drift. *The Cognitive Behaviour Therapist*, 14, E37. https://doi.org/10.1017/S1754470X21000350

Part II

Creating solid foundations

Chapter 9

Establishing a basic structure

Introduction

The key aim of Part I was to acquaint CBT supervisors with some of the most influential models of therapist skill development that underpin our work with supervisees. A thorough understanding of what we are supposed to be doing as supervisors can help us when we come to design the architecture of our supervision sessions and when we come to review how well we adhere to the core tasks within our role. Having acquired some technical knowledge about supervision, it is important to get off to a good start when working with supervisees, therefore ensuring that 'solid foundations' are in place to facilitate supervisee skill development is paramount. The key aim of Part II is to help CBT supervisors put in place a set of practices that represent these solid foundations. This chapter uses the analogy of building a house with supervision methods being the internal 'furnishings', meta-supervision acting as the 'roof of the house' and three influential frameworks – the Supervisor competences (Roth & Pilling, 2008), the 'tandem model' (Milne & Dunkerley, 2010) and Gordon's ten steps (Gordon, 2012) that I will refer to as the 'pillars' that hold supervision together.

It is beyond the scope of this chapter to discuss each of these structures in detail and readers are encouraged to access supporting literature that can provide a richer account of each. What follows is a snapshot of each pillar, and how they can be used to support the rationale for selecting different supervision methods to meet the needs of each supervisee at any given time. Finally, it is proposed that the key factor which maintains supervisory structure is the supervision question, as this provides a window into the supervisee's knowledge, skills and reflective capacity.

Pillar 1: Supervisor competences

Roth and Pilling (2007) developed a competence framework for the training of psychological therapies with the UK, one of which focused on CBT. In relation to this, they also devised a set of competences to support supervisor training (Roth & Pilling, 2008) These competences are made up of four domains – generic (e.g. help the supervisee present information about clinical work), specific (e.g. incorporate

DOI: 10.4324/9781003590620-11

direct observation into supervision), modality specific (e.g. applied to the practice of CBT) and meta competences (e.g. adapt the process and conduct of supervision based on the experience of the supervisee).

This list of competences has been derived from a literature review and expert consensus and whilst it represents a thorough consideration of what contributes to effective supervision, it can be difficult to remember all of these in the middle of a supervision session. For this reason, we need a way of simplifying these concepts so that they are more easily recalled.

Pillar 2: The tandem model

Derek Milne and colleagues have written extensively on CBT supervision, and the culmination of their research lies in the tandem model and the supervisor competence measures that are linked to this – the Supervision: Adherence and Guidance Evaluation Scale (SAGE) and, more recently, the short-SAGE (Milne & Reiser, 2014; Reiser et al., 2018). In summary, the tandem model proposes that the supervisor and supervisee are likened to two cyclists riding a tandem bike. The supervisor sits at the front of the bike and is responsible for pedalling and turning the front wheel, whilst the supervisee sits at the back and operates the real wheel.

The concept of the supervisor and supervisee as cyclists riding a tandem bike is easy to visualise, and to build on this metaphor, supervision that is drifting is likely to be characterised by very few 'front' or 'real wheel' wheel' behaviours. In this book, the tandem bike analogy will be used more flexibly to explain how supervision that is 'on track' is characterised by the supervision dyad 'peddling in the same direction'. This leads on to the concepts that I refer to as supervision supporting behaviours (SSBS) and supervision-interfering behaviours (SIBS).

Table 9.1 Examples of supervisor and supervisee behaviours within the tandem model (based on Milne & Dunkerley, 2010)

Front wheel 'Supervisor behaviours' examples	*Rear wheel 'Supervisee behaviours'*
Demonstrating	Experiencing
	Reflecting
Evaluating Experiencing	Conceptualising
	Planning
Formulating	
	Experimenting (5 in total)
Observing Training (18 in total)	

Supervisor tip

SSBs can be embedded through the consistent use of supervisory methods that are linked to Pillars 1 and 2, whilst SIBS can be initiated or maintained by either the supervisor or the supervisee.

SSBS

Holding this concept in mind, if the supervisor is attending to the formative aspects of their role then they are steering the bike along a path of learning. With trainees, this is helping them to consolidate declarative and procedural knowledge about various models and interventions. With qualified therapists, the steering is often to reduce the risk of 'therapist drift' (Waller, 2009) or to help them navigate more challenging cases. If a meta-supervisor was to observe a supervision session recording, they would be looking to observe certain skills that suggest that the supervisor is engaging in SSBS. For example, the SAGE as mentioned earlier, can be used to measure the degree to which any one of eighteen supervisor behaviours are present in any given supervision session.

Reflective exercise

Bring to mind one supervisee who seems to be 'peddling in the same direction' as you

Describe their supervision supporting behaviours that signal to you that you are aligned with them on the tasks and goals for supervision?

Now bring to a mind a supervisee where there is/was less of a shared understanding of the direction of travel

What are/were the supervision-interfering behaviours displayed by either party?

Pillar 3: Gordon's ten steps

The journal paper by Gordon (2012) presents a fine example of how one might structure a supervision session, centred around a list of ten supervision supporting behaviours. The aim of this paper according to Gordon is to provide 'a bridge to link the complexities of guidelines and models of supervision to their moment-by-moment facilitation of the supervision meeting' (p72). A description of all ten steps is beyond the scope of this chapter, therefore readers are encouraged to access the paper directly. Here, I focus on one of the key supervisee behaviours which help the supervisor to adapt the session to their current needs. What I am referring to is the supervision question, which encapsulates the particular aspect of theory or practice in which the supervisee requires support.

Developing a good supervision question (SQ)

Experience suggests that developing a good supervision question is easier said than done. As a supervisor, it is important for us to understand what our supervisees wish to get from a particular supervision session. When we set the agenda, we usually ask for which cases they would like to discuss and what their question is. It is not uncommon for trainees (and some qualified therapists) to launch into providing copious amount of background information about the client, which does not always reveal what they wish to learn. It is our job as supervisors to help them in learning how to develop good SQs. I would go as far to say that effective supervision hinges on how well the supervisor is able to help their supervisee in refining the SQ.

The functions of the supervision question

The SQ serves a range of functions for both the supervisor and supervisee. From the supervisor's perspective, it helps with managing time, especially in a group format. Setting the agenda when there are three or four supervisees in a group can 'eat into' the time available for actually answering the question therefore it is crucial that questions are refined as quickly as possible.

Being able to provide a succinct question relatively quickly, helps to get the supervision agenda set and the supervisor to get on with helping to answer the question itself. It is also a window into the supervisee's stage of development as a therapist. For example, if we consider the Integrative Developmental Model (IDM) stages (see Chapter 6) and categories of skill development (e.g. case conceptualisation skills) the clarity and form of the SQ can gives clues as to where the focus of supervision needs to be (Stoltenberg & McNeill, 2010). We can also hold in mind the components of the Declarative Procedural Reflective (DPR) model (see Chapter 5) when considering the declarative knowledge and procedural skills of the supervisee (Bennett-Levy, 2006).

> As both Tom and Sonny are relatively new to CBT, many of their questions relate to differential diagnosis and understanding which models to use with their clients (declarative knowledge). For Basma and Trudie, they tend to bring questions related to barriers that seem to arise once they have implemented models in treatment (procedural skills).

From the supervisee's perspective, the SQ can help them to focus on what they specifically need to get from the current supervision session. This can help them to decide how many clients they can realistically present in one supervision session and also, which supervision method is best suited to each case.

Developing effective supervision questions

Rather than viewing supervision questions as 'good' or 'bad', we can think of them in terms of levels of effectiveness. Less effective supervision questions tend to be rather vague as shown in the following vignette. Ramesh has previously struggled with generating SMART SQ's in his own supervision and therefore has been working on improving this skill within meta-supervision. In the following vignette, Ramesh is practising helping Tom to refine his SQ.

Ramesh: So, Tom what are your agenda items for supervision today?
Tom: I've got a PTSD client and I'm not really sure what I'm doing with them.
Ramesh: Ok, when you say not really sure what you are doing, can you be more specific?
Tom: I've never worked with PTSD before so I'm not sure where to start.
Ramesh: That's understandable. It would help me to understand what you mean by where to start. Are you talking about formulating or starting treatment?

This interaction highlights how Tom has failed to prepare ahead of the supervision session with Ramesh. He uses rather global terms such as 'not sure what I'm doing' which makes it difficult for Ramesh to know if this relates to his declarative knowledge of PTSD or his confidence in using his procedural skills to formulate or begin using interventions with his client.

In contrast, more effective SQs follow the well-established SMART principles (specific, measurable, achievable, realistic and time-based). The following vignette shows how Basma prepared a specific SQ and how her supervisor Ramesh helped to make it measurable, achievable, realistic and time based.

Ramesh: What is your question in relation to this client?
Basma: Yeah so, I'm working with a client with PTSD, and I've gone through the formulation with them and they seem to get it, but I'm not sure how to start the process of reliving.
Ramesh: Ok, so it sounds as if your question is around how to introduce reliving or how to actually start it with the client?
Basma: I've explained it to them, I'm just not sure where to start in the memory and what to do if they freak out during the reliving.
Ramesh: Got you. So it sounds as if there are two questions there Basma – the first being a technical question around at what point in the memory to start reliving and the second is maybe some therapist fears around how the client will react during reliving?
Basma: Yeah that's right.

This interaction shows how Basma has prepared a specific question about reliving, however, Ramesh helps to make it even more specific by asking questions to clarify what the focus for the session will be. Following the SMART acronym in order, the next part of managing the question is to measure how effectively it has been answered. However, Ramesh might first want to determine if it is realistic and achievable to address both aspects of her question within this supervision session.

Ramesh: Ok, so I'm conscious of the time we have, so it might not be possible to address both of those questions today. You've got about 40 minutes, so are there any other cases you wanted to review today?

Basma: No, just this one.

Ramesh: Ok, so what feels like the most pressing issue, is it where to start in the memory or is it the fear of the client getting too distressed?

Basma: I think it's a bit of both to be honest. I think where we start in the memory might determine the level of distress.

Ramesh: Ok, let's review your formulation so we can see how the memory fits with their wider presenting problems and consider in the first instance where it makes most sense to start with memory processing.

The supervisor would then pick a supervision method that takes account of the supervisee's declarative knowledge and procedural skill. In this instance, Ramesh chose to model how to start memory processing and then asked Basma to swap roles and replicate what he had shown her. It is then vital to review the learning that has taken place and to consider what 'homework' the supervisee could do to build on this (e.g. further skills practice or reading a journal paper).

Preparing the SQ

We can (wrongly) assume that supervisees know how to prepare for supervision, yet anecdotal experience suggests that this is something that many trainees struggle with, especially if prior experiences of supervision have been very different. For example, supervision might have been a review of one's full caseload or an open reflection on thoughts and feelings that arise when working with specific clients. Qualified therapists can also struggle with providing clear supervision questions or their questions might continue to be restricted to certain aspects of a case (e.g. technical questions) rather than including aspects such as reflecting on alliance difficulties (Moorey & Lavender, 2019). In these instances, a supervision preparation worksheet such as the one developed by Padesky (2005) can be helpful to give to supervisees in advance of the session.

Supervisor tip

Asking supervisees to email their SQ to you ahead of the session can help to focus them on what exactly they need and also saves times when setting the agenda.

Barriers to developing effective SQ's

If a supervisee continues to bring vague SQs or appears to expect you as the supervisor to tell them what to do at each stage with their clients, it might be worthwhile putting this on the agenda for specific exploration. There could be time pressures, which mean that the supervisee only starts to formulate a SQ a few minutes before meeting with you. Alternatively, the supervisee might experience considerable self-doubt in relation to their case conceptualisation skills or application of specific techniques. It can be useful to 'name the elephant in the room' if this becomes a pattern across supervision sessions. Appendix 2 provides a handy checklist that can be given to supervisees to assist them in preparing for supervision sessions.

Maintaining structure

Using one or more of the three frameworks that were described earlier as the 'foundations' of our supervisory practice can help us to maintain structure when there is the risk of drift. With trainees, it is these foundations that support skill development and with qualified therapists, these same foundations help to support continual skill enhancement throughout their career. Figure 9.1 provides a visual representation of the house-building analogy. In addition to the supporting pillars, a range of 'building blocks' help to maintain the structure of CBT supervision and these include:

- A contract
- A 'good enough' working alliance
- Appropriate methods for assessing learning and competence
- Agreement on what to do if supervision begins to 'drift' from its core functions
- Regular reviews to check if supervision remains effective

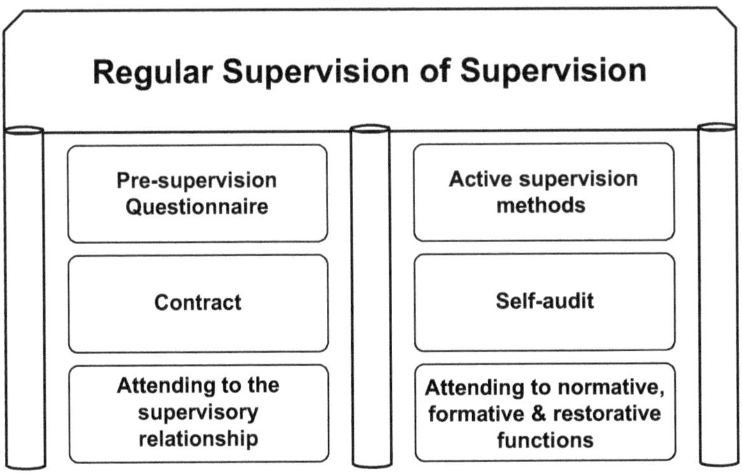

Figure 9.1 Building a stable home for supervision.

Contract

Beyond the physical 'terms and conditions' of a supervision contract, a 'psychological contract (Clohessy, 2019) is developed that takes account of key personal and professional background factors (e.g. social GRRRAAACCEEESSS, stage of the supervisee's development, their preferences, strengths and weaknesses and their 'alignment' with CBT (Burnham, 2012; Roscoe & Wilbraham, 2024; Stoltenberg & McNeill, 2010). This can be supported through the use of a pre-supervision questionnaire which will discussed in more detail in Chapter 10.

A 'good enough' working alliance

For supervision to be effective there needs to be a 'good enough' working alliance, which is characterised by the 'bond' between supervisor and supervisee and sufficient agreement on the key tasks and goals for each session (see Bordin, 1983). This does not mean getting on like friends, in fact, in supervisory relationships where it feels like this, there is a risk of supervision losing some of its formality and potentially, its normative functions (Proctor, 1994). Good enough means that the supervisee feels safe to share their work and that power is managed within the relationship. Beyond this, there should be explicit agreement on what methods will be used and how these align with the agreed goals.

We need to create opportunities for mutual feedback within supervision therefore it important to agree a session where goals can be reviewed and adjusted. It is also important that we invite open and honest feedback on our supervisory skills, therefore it is helpful to administer one or more outcome measures at regular intervals (see Chapter 12).

Appropriate methods for assessing learning and competence

Active methods such as reviewing recordings of the supervisees work and skills practice in the form of supervisor modelling and role-play are often the best ways to help the supervisee to continue to learn and grow as a therapist. Chapters 13–20 provide a wide range of examples of how we can use active methods to support supervisee skill development.

Agreement on what to do if supervision begins to 'drift' from its core functions

Another key element is having a mechanism or mechanisms in place for monitoring supervision (e.g. evaluating how well the supervisor supports, evaluates and guides the supervisee). This is likely to be different from standard supervision satisfaction questionnaires. This might include the agreement to formulate supervisee avoidance or for the supervision dyad to reflect on how often they are using active methods in comparison to case discussion.

Regular reviews to check if supervision remains effective

Regular Supervision of Supervision (SoS) or meta-supervision, provides the supervisor with a more consistent way of reviewing their supervisory skills, with the benefit of having another 'set of eyes' on their work. SoS could include formal reviews of supervisor skills using measures such as the Supervision Adherence and Guidance Evaluation (SAGE) or short SAGE (see Milne et al., 2011; Reiser et al., 2018).

Supervision-Interfering Behaviours

For a variety of reasons, the supervisor or supervisee may at times, engage in behaviours that are supervision interfering rather than supervision supporting. This is likely to happen even if all of the above components are in place given that human beings are wonderfully imperfect. Poor or absent SQs that persist over time are one example of SIBS. This topic will be addressed in more detail within Chapter 18. The methods that are described in the rest of Part II and Part III can help to limit the presence and influence of SIBS, however, should they persist, there are a range of tools that can be deployed by the supervisor to address this.

Questions for meta-supervision

My supervisee and I seem to have very different ideas about what supervision is for. How can I address this without causing a rupture?

My supervisee turns up to every supervision session without a clear question. What should I do to support them with this?

Chapter summary

- The Roth and Pilling Supervisor Competence Framework offers a comprehensive guide to effective supervision, though it could be challenging to apply in real-time without simplification.
- The Tandem bike model offers a simple way of explaining the 'supervision journey'.
- Gordon's Ten Steps provides a practical, step-by-step guide to structuring supervision sessions. This can be useful for auditing supervision quality and minimising supervisory drift.

- A well-developed SQ helps the supervisor manage time, understand the supervisee's developmental stage (e.g. via IDM and DPR models) and tailor the supervision methods accordingly.
- Both trainees and qualified therapists may struggle with SQs due to varied past supervision experiences. Developing effective SQs is a skill that requires practice rather than something that improves purely from years of experience as a therapist.
- SoS can be thought of as the 'roof' that contains all of the processes within effective supervision and keeps the foundations 'in place'.

Recommended reading

Gordon, P. K. (2012). Ten steps to cognitive behavioural supervision. *Cognitive Behaviour Therapist*, 5.

Chapter 10

Starting well

Going beyond the paper contract

Introduction

'Fail to prepare, prepare to fail' is a saying that often comes to mind when setting up behavioural experiments with clients. Without taking the time to establish the client's understanding of the rationale for the experiment or having vague predictions about the outcome and what they will learn from the experience, there is a considerable risk of things not going to plan. This is also true when entering into a new supervisory relationship, whereby taking the time to establish 'solid foundations' from the offset will pay dividends in the long run.

When I reflect upon some of the most difficult supervisory relationships that I have been part of, one of the common denominators is a lack of preparation when first starting to work with the supervisee. Of course, contracting is a key part of that preparation, and most readers will be familiar with a written supervision contract that both parties read and sign. The written contract is often a list of the 'terms and conditions' set out by the supervisor or the organisation in which they work. This usually includes aspects of the supervision arrangement, such as frequency of meeting, location, requirements for supplying recordings of clinical work, payment and what to do with regards to cancellations or terminating the agreement.

The purpose of contracting

Contracting serves a range of functions (e.g. having a shared understanding of roles and responsibilities) and acts as a reference point should either party wish to change the terms or seek to clarify expectations. Common amendments to supervision contracts might include changes to the frequency of meeting, the goals of the supervisee or the fee that is charged if this takes place in PP. When I think about my own challenges or those that supervisors have brought to me in meta-supervision, the presence of a written contract is rarely the issue. Problems have arisen when we have 'dived' straight into doing supervision, rather than taking the time to clarify each other's expectations of the process, and of the other person's role throughout this period of time working together. This chapter is concerned with taking contracting beyond these administrative tasks. Instead, a more collaborative and relational form of contracting will be introduced.

DOI: 10.4324/9781003590620-12

The macro and micro skills of contracting

We can view contracting as consisting of both 'macro' and 'micro' level skills (James et al., 2008). At the macro level, the key skill is ensuring that the foundations are in place for a solid working alliance. Bordin's (1983) model of the alliance is often referenced in supervision training and literature and consists of

- An agreement on the goals of supervision
- Agreement on the associated tasks to be undertaken during supervision sessions
- A good enough 'bond' or alliance between supervisor and supervisee

Anticipating areas that require a particular focus within supervision

At the micro level, contracting helps to ensure that supervision is tailored to the developmental needs of the supervisee. Part of being a more dynamic supervisor is anticipating the idiosyncratic needs of each supervisee. Taking the time to do this at the start of a supervisory relationship means that we are in a better position to tailor supervision to the individual (e.g. by anticipating which supervision methods are most suited to their current needs). Tailoring supervision involves a consideration of:

- Learning styles/preferences (e.g. visual, kinaesthetic)
- Length of qualification/Integrative Developmental Model (IDM) stage (Stoltenberg, 1981)
- Asking about past experiences of supervision and preferences around content and feedback
- Anticipating the supervisee's 'Achilles heel' in therapy and supervision (e.g. having demanding standards)
- Anticipating role transition difficulties

Addressing 'silent assumptions'

In addition to making supervision more specific to the supervisee, contracting helps to identify the silent assumptions that supervisees carry about their role and that of their supervisor within supervision sessions. Both supervisor and supervisee enter into the supervisory relationship holding a range of assumptions about each other's roles, responsibilities and goals during their work together. Whilst the paper contract helps to name some of these, there are aspects that often go unsaid. This might relate to the presumption that both parties are 'singing from the same hymn sheet'. Furthermore, expectations of how each party will behave within the relationship are often silent, guided by past experiences of supervision.

Table 10.1 provides some examples of rules and expectations that CBT supervisors and supervisees might hold about the *process* of supervision and about what

Table 10.1 Unspoken rules or expectations in supervision

Supervisee	*Supervisor*
• My supervisor *should* provide me with all the answers • The supervisor will tell me what we can use the time for	• The supervisee *should* read books and papers rather than just relying on supervision for the answers • The supervisee will prepare adequately for the supervision session and know what they want to find out

they believe are the *responsibilities* of the other person. Whilst these might be verbalised on occasions, research suggests that these are often unspoken (Roscoe et al., 2022a).

What these examples highlight is that the supervisor and supervisee may hold very different beliefs about what either other will or won't do or should do. We can see that without expressing these expectations openly, there is the risk of conflict arising sooner or later within the supervisory relationship.

Reflective exercise

Do you make time to explore your supervisee's supervision history and/or expectations of supervision?

Using a Pre-Supervision Questionnaire (PSQ)

The concept of 'psychological contracting' was brought to my attention when I attended a supervisor training event some years back (Clohessy, 2019). The training was about improving the supervisory relationship, and some ideas were given about the types of questions one might ask at the start of the relationship which would facilitate strong communication between the supervision dyad. I quickly became enthused about using this with my supervisees and, in hindsight, wished I had asked ex-supervisees these questions too.

I put together a questionnaire that drew upon some of the questions in this workshop and added some others that I thought expanded the enquiry. I subsequently piloted this questionnaire, which I refer to as the Pre-Supervision Questionnaire (PSQ) at numerous workshops that I presented on CBT Supervision over several years, adapting the content based on participant feedback and further supervisory experiences. I have since created three versions: one for use with trainees, one for qualified supervisees and one for use within Supervision of Supervision (SoS). I cannot emphasise enough how fruitful this exercise is when it is done well, and it has been extremely well received by many workshop participants who have shared with me the many ways in which it has helped them when applying it in their own supervisory relationships.

Not only is the PSQ helpful for illuminating some of the beliefs (e.g. rules and assumptions) that govern our expectations of supervision, it also promotes self-reflection and openness from supervisees about their strengths, weaknesses and any factors that might generate difficulties for them in their clinical work (e.g. working with PTSD cases when they have also suffered from PTSD in the past).

PSQ sections

The PSQ consists of three parts (A, B & C). Part A is concerned with understanding personal factors (e.g. identifying key aspects of the supervisee's identity; gauging awareness of strengths and weaknesses, preferences) and one's previous professional role (e.g. how closely aligned this was with the principles and practices of CBT). This can open up a dialogue about lived experience of mental health problems, neurodiversity and experiences of discrimination, all of which can be helpful for both supervisee and supervisor when planning supervision content (Laville et al., 2025; Limper-Menapace, 2025). It can also help the supervision dyad to consider some of the challenges that are associated with role transition, such as struggling to let go of old ways of working (Robinson et al., 2012; Wilcockson, 2020). In contrast, Part B seeks to understand preferred supervision methods whereby supervisees highlight or circle ones they have used in the past or are interested in using going forward.

Finally, Part C is concerned with negotiating how to provide and elicit feedback within the supervisory relationship. This helps the supervisor to understand the best way of evaluating the supervisory alliance (e.g. agreeing on how often supervision outcome or alliance measures might be used) and managing any tension or disagreement within the relationship, such as how to spot signs of a rupture.

Table 10.2 Example questions within a pre-supervision questionnaire (adapted for qualified therapists)

Part A: Understanding salient background information

- What would you say are your strengths and weaknesses as a CBT practitioner?
- How would you feel about discussing factors that influence how you see yourself and the world? (e.g. race, gender, sexuality, etc.)

Part B: Methods for developing and enhancing skills

- In relation to reviewing audio or video recordings of your therapy sessions, how do you feel about this?

Part C: Managing the relationship

- How would you like to provide feedback to me on my supervisory style/skill?

Whilst this information could be elicited during a live supervision session, writing down answers ahead of an initial meeting gives the supervisee time to consider how much detail they wish to provide at this stage.

> **Supervisor tip**
>
> This can be particularly useful for supervisees with neurodiversity or those with lived experience of mental health problems who might feel uneasy about discussing this 'on the spot'.

Exploring attitudes towards active supervision methods

I usually ask the supervisee to email me their completed PSQ ahead of our first meeting, as it allows me to target my follow-up questions based on the responses given. Their responses to Part B offer clues about their receptiveness towards various supervision methods. For example, supervisees are asked to highlight or circle any methods that are of interest to them, and any methods that are not circled should evoke curiosity within the supervisor as to why this might be. When reviewing this in session, it is important to embody this curious stance as shown in the vignette below.

Sonia: Thanks for filling in the PSQ. How did you find the experience?
Sonny: It was ok, quite useful to reflect on what I have enjoyed previously in supervision and what I didn't enjoy that much.
Sonia: Yes, quite a few of my supervisees have said they found it helpful to reflect on strengths, weaknesses and challenges in past supervisory relationships. Which methods did you enjoy?
Sonny: It was good to get to know what my supervisor would do in my situation so, I always found their advice about cases invaluable.
Sonia: I see, and what didn't you do much of in the past?
Sonny: Role-play! I'm glad really. It just doesn't feel natural so I would go along with it at the time but didn't really find it helpful.

By reviewing key responses to the PSQ questions, Sonia was able to understand Sonny's preference for advice seeking. This discussion also identified negative attitudes towards role-play. Sonia went on to explore what the role-play had been used for, how it was introduced and if feedback was elicited from the supervisee at the time. Sonia was then able to correct some misconceptions about role-play and ask the supervisee for permission to use it in future, should a supervision question lend itself to this method. In terms of the over-reliance on advice seeking, Sonia recognised that this was a legacy from Sonny's previous supervision but also very common amongst IDM Level 1 therapists (Stoltenberg & McNeill, 2010). Sonia made a note to explore this again later in his training to see if he was starting to display behaviour that is more typical of those at Level 2.

Modifying Supervision Schemas

As highlighted in previous chapters, CBT therapists (or Clinical Psychologists like Sonny, who are also doing a CBT pathway) commence their training having been supervised in previous professional roles (e.g. social work, mental health nursing) and this will, in part, influence their expectations of what supervision consists of. The supervision they receive during training and post qualification further adds to the 'supervision schema' that is in development (e.g. reinforces or challenges).

Whilst some supervisees will be very open to a new style of supervision, others will experience some level of discomfort or 'schematic resistance' around core tasks such as showing video recordings or being more structured in how they use the time available.

> As we saw earlier in the book, Trudie had come to see supervision as a place to offload and to discuss the challenges of her caseload or the demands of the organisation. Conversely, Sonia's supervisory schema was that supervision is a place to learn and grow as a therapist. This means there is a high risk of a schematic mismatch between Trudie and Sonia. The PSQ provides them with a means of discussing what they each expect to get from supervision and to negotiate how they can develop a structure that best supports Trudie's development.

If supervisees have experienced supervision that was dominated by verbal discussion in the past, they might expect more of the same. Likewise, supervisees who have experienced harmful supervision could be hypervigilant for signs that they are in danger in this relationship.

> Tom's previous experiences of supervision were in the form of case management, and he found his previous supervisor, a senior Psychological Wellbeing Practitioner (PWP), to be emotionally cold and only focused on attaining service targets.

The PSQ creates the opportunity to air these types of concerns, and the supervisor can summarise the key points that are written within the document, collaborating with the supervisee to plan for how they manage session content and emotional reactions going forward.

Summarising salient information

Just as you might create a case summary sheet to provide a birds eye view of a new client, it can be helpful to succinctly extrapolate salient information from the PSQ and from your early interactions with a supervisee. Whilst there are no specific rules about how much detail to extrapolate, it seems sensible to list some bullet points about the key strengths and weaknesses of the supervisee, together with areas of interest and things to watch out for in subsequent meetings. Table 10.3 offers an example of Basma's salient information as summarised by her supervisor Ramesh. The salient information captured about Basma is a fairly detailed version; therefore, it is important to hold in mind that the level of detail and self-awareness will vary considerably amongst supervisees. Furthermore, it might take longer for the supervisor to populate the form with this level of detail (e.g. over several months). An additional consideration is that it could feel difficult for supervisees to raise sensitive issues within group supervision. Appendix 3 provides some advice on general adaptations that might be needed in a group context.

Table 10.4 provides an example of a Supervisee Summary Record. This could also be a helpful document to review within one's supervision of supervision (SoS)

Table 10.3 Salient information captured within the PSQ

Key strengths	*Formulating using disorder-specific models for anxiety disorders; forming effective working relationships with clients*
Key areas for development	*Consistent use of outcome measures (e.g. PHQ-9); Longitudinal Formulation (especially rules and assumptions)*
Preferred methods within supervision	*Supervisor modelling; reviewing videos; self-practice of CBT*
Least favourite methods within supervision	*Role-Play*
Salient background information	*Trained later in life, feels quite maternal towards younger female clients and co-workers*
Potential therapy-interfering beliefs and behaviours	*It's rude to interrupt clients* *Missing longitudinal data when presenting cases*
Potential supervision-interfering beliefs and behaviours	*Dislikes exercises that make her feel 'uncomfortable'*

Table 10.4 Example supervisee summary record – Basma

Supervisee Initials _BA___
Frequency of Supervision __*Monthly*_________
Level of CBT Training __*Post Graduate Diploma*_________
Length of time qualified __*1 year* _________
Approximate Overall IDM Level __Overall 2; ________

Relevant Personal Information as agreed with the supervisee

Relevant Previous/Current Professional Information that might impact on the supervisee's alignment with CBT

(*Continued*)

Table 10.4 (Continued)

Current Goals for Supervision:
Date of next review:
Potential Challenges to the Supervisory Alliance

and can also be used to support a self-directed auditing process. This could be contained within one document to include the salient information in Table 10.3 and could also include the IDM snapshot in Chapter 6 (see Appendix 6).

Questions for meta-supervision

My supervisee has not ticked any of the active methods options on the PSQ, how should I address this?

I'm not sure how to adapt to supervision in light of some of the information my supervisee has put on the PSQ. Should I tell them this?

Chapter summary

- This chapter aims to help CBT supervisors to get off to as good a start as possible with their supervisees through creating opportunities to discuss salient information.
- It can be helpful to spend time understanding previous supervisory relationships, the styles that the supervisee has been exposed to and the methods that have been utilised.
- Having some awareness of this will help supervisors to develop shared goals and to anticipate challenges from the offset.

Recommended reading

Beinart, H. (2014). Building and sustaining the supervisory relationship. In Watkins Jr, C. E. & Milne, D. L. (Eds.) *The Wiley international handbook of clinical supervision*. John Wiley & Sons.

Chapter 11

Addressing difference and diversity

Introduction

In recent years there has been an increased recognition of the need to ensure that CBT is culturally sensitive, and where appropriate, culturally adapted (Beck, 2016). Research has indicated that CBT therapists often lack confidence in this aspect of their work (Presley, 2025) and training around cultural competence varies considerably in scope and quality (see Faheem, 2023). Supervision is the ideal environment for discussing issues related to difference and diversity that affect supervisees and their clients (Pieterse et al., 2025). For example, opening up conversations on topics such as racism, homophobia and experiences of 'micro aggressions' (e.g. behaviours that are often covert yet communicate derogatory or hostile messages: Sue et al., 2019) has the potential to support supervisees in processing their emotional reactions to challenging situations or through recognising structural disadvantages (Black & Stone, 2005). This allyship can help supervisees to work through their fears about raising issues related to different protected characteristics such as ethnicity and sexuality (e.g. saying the wrong thing and offending the client; Laville et al., 2025).

Understanding barriers to culturally sensitive supervision

CBT supervision may not be fulfilling its potential in this regard, as some supervisors might be worried about bringing up these topics themselves during supervision (e.g. 'what if the supervisee thinks I'm making a big issue of their sexuality/ethnicity/gender identity'). There is also the possibility that a supervisor is passive and waits for supervisees to bring up these topics (e.g. 'if it's important to them they will tell me'). Another possibility is that the supervisor is ignorant to their many privileges (e.g. shows 'colour blindness) and therefore it does not even cross their mind to put these items on their agenda (Williams et al., 2022).

DOI: 10.4324/9781003590620-13

Reflective exercise

Q. How often do you explicitly discuss areas of similarity and difference between the supervisee and yourself?
Q. At what point in the supervisory relationship is this discussed?

Making room for discussions about differences within supervision

This chapter will briefly address how supervisors can overcome these barriers by providing some examples of how supervision can be used to actively support supervisees' learning and development in relation to difference and diversity. The Pre-Supervision Questionnaire (PSQ; see Chapter 10) is a natural 'in road' for these types of discussions, as it invites supervisees to provide salient information about aspects of their personal and previous professional identities. Administering this at the start of a supervisory relationship (SR) opens the door for discussing similarities and differences between the supervisor and the supervisee. Certain aspects of difference and diversity will be visible (e.g. skin colour), whereas others might be less visible, as is the case for Tom.

> Tom was still trying to make sense of his sexual orientation and whilst he identified as a gay man, he had not told most of his family, friends or work colleagues. Tom recognised that he struggled to work with clients who were also struggling to feel fully comfortable with their sexuality, but he did not want to share this aspect of his identity with his supervisor Ramesh. Tom struggled with the heteronormative assumptions within his team at work as many of his colleagues assumed he was heterosexual and would ask him why he hasn't got a girlfriend.

Clearly, there is little that Ramesh can do directly to support Tom if he is unaware of his sexual orientation, and how his internal conflict affects his clinical work. The aim is not to encourage Tom to 'come out' through using the PSQ. Instead, what Ramesh can do in this scenario is ensure that he does not fall into using the same heteronormative assumptions as Tom's other work colleagues. He can also demonstrate to Tom that he thinks and works in an inclusive way by showing an interest in Tom's personal reactions to clients rather than just commenting on techniques and protocols.

The salient circles exercise

The salient circles exercise (Buchanan, 2020) is a natural follow-on from reviewing the main points that have been captured within the PSQ. This exercise can be used to help supervisees feel that all parts of their identity are important and seen, and it can also highlight key differences in how the supervisor and supervisee view the world.

To begin, the supervisor would explain that we all have salient aspects of what make us who we are, some of which are visible to the world (e.g. the colour of our skin) and some of which are invisible or less visible (e.g. our sexual orientation). The key here is that supervisees share what they are comfortable with others knowing (e.g. Tom might not wish to draw a circle for every part of his identity). The salient circles exercise can be helpful for at least two reasons. Firstly, it enables the supervision dyad to get to know each other, which helps with general rapport building, and secondly, it helps the supervisor to know where the supervisee might need restorative input or support in managing difficult situations within their clinical work. Table 11.1 shows an excerpt from Basma's PSQ, which highlights an aspect of her clinical work which might require additional restorative attention at various points.

If Basma was subject to racism from a client during their work together, Ramesh might ask if she wanted to discuss this within supervision. The salient circles exercise can also point supervisors towards the language and metaphors that best suit their supervisee, as the vignette involving Sonia and Sonny demonstrates.

> Sonia suggested to Sonny that they both complete the salient circles exercise within supervision (see Figure 11.1). Once they had each drawn this out, they compared and contrasted both the aspects of their identity that were salient to them, and the respective size and positioning of each circle. As the diagrams show, gender is more salient to Sonia than it is to Sonny, however ethnicity is more salient to Sonny than to Sonia. This reflects how individuals can have a complex mix of areas of privilege and disadvantage. Other key differences are in relation to religion and parenthood. Other than their shared career path, Sonia and Sonny both have an interest in sport with Sonia being a keen runner and Sonny a keen football supporter. An awareness of this can also help with the types of metaphors that one uses in supervision. For example, Sonia could use football-based metaphors to support feedback when working with Sonny and this might be less appropriate for another supervisee who dislikes football.

Table 11.1 Excerpt from Basma's PSQ responses

Is there any personal or professional background information about you that you think is important for me to know?
As a Muslim woman I have been subjected to verbal abuse from both clients and members of the public. This means that I can be quite anxious about working with clients that hold certain political views. I also feel really angry and over-identify with other Muslims who have been abused. This means that I can struggle to step away from my involvement in certain cases.

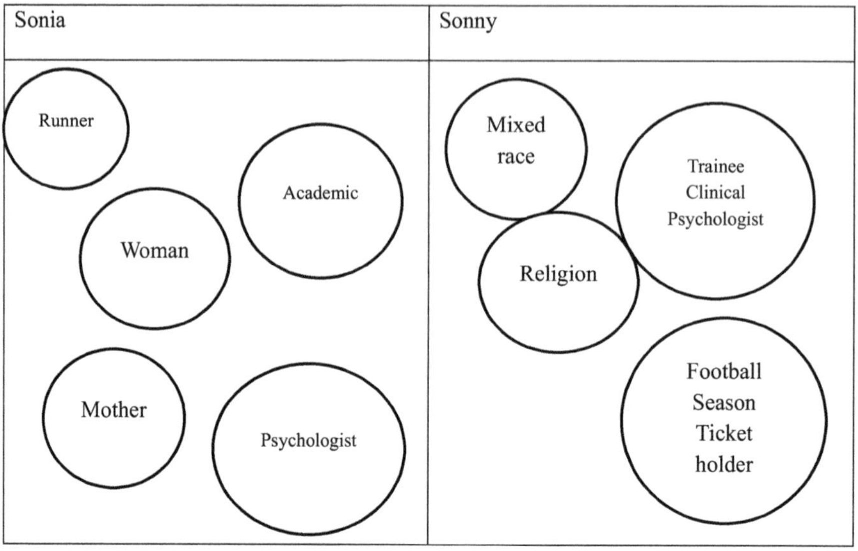

Figure 11.1 Example of a completed salient circles exercise.

Holding this information in mind

The salient circles exercise helps the supervision dyad to anticipate areas where they might need to play closer attention within supervision. For example, knowing about the salience of Basma's ethnicity and religion as part of her identity, can shape discussions when she brings clients who share this. The exercise can also help supervisors to consider where they might occasionally get things wrong and which may trigger a rupture. For example, failing to acknowledge a religious festival or showing ignorance to world events such as the Black Lives Matter movement.

> **Supervisor tip**
>
> It is crucial that this exercise is not undertaken in a tokenistic way, whereby it is never revisited in supervision. Completing this exercise and referring back to it in future sessions show the supervisee that you are willing to reflect on aspects of their identity (and your own) in a meaningful way.

Understanding intersectionality

For some supervisees or their clients, several areas of disadvantage can 'intersect', whereby there is a much greater risk of them experiencing discrimination, hate or trauma (Crenshaw, 1989). The term 'intersectionality' captures this, and supervision can also help supervisees to reflect on how they might modify their assessments, formulations and interventions to take account of the effects of intersectionality.

> The salient circles exercise helped Tom to see that as a white, British, cisgender male, there are many aspects of his identity that he pays little or no attention to in day-to-day life. Seeing that ethnicity and religion were two larger circles on his supervisor Ramesh's diagram made Tom reflect on how he tends to overlook many aspects of intersectionality when formulating cases. Further discussion about Tom's personal history revealed that he had grown up in a small rural village and had not interacted with many individuals who were significantly different to himself in terms of ethnicity or religion.

Ramesh: Tom, in light of these reflections after completing the salient circles exercise, I wondered if we might spend some time today thinking about how we can develop your cultural competences even further. What would you think about that?

Tom: I know it's important and we can do if you want, it's just that I had a case that I really wanted your opinion on . . . . .I'm seeing the client again tomorrow.

Ramesh: Ok, maybe we could put both items on the agenda and see how best to split the time?

Tom: Yeah sounds like a plan.

Supervisees like Tom might need some gentle encouragement to start adding factors relating to intersectionality within their supervision questions. It is also important to explore Tom's reactions to these suggestions.

Ramesh: Maybe it's just me but something seemed to change in your body language when I suggested putting cultural competence on the agenda. What is going through your mind right now?

Tom: I don't know . . . . I guess I feel a bit silly. Now you point these things out, I realise that because these things don't affect me, I don't ask my clients about them.

Ramesh: It's really good that you have that awareness but try not to be too self-critical Tom. I have certain blind spots too when I am doing assessments and developing formulations.

Tom: The client I am bringing today . . . . .I definitely haven't thought enough about their sexual orientation and how some of their experiences of homophobia might affect how they feel in social situations.

Ramesh: Ok, if we mapped out the formulation for your client with intersectional factors included, how might that change your conceptualisation of their difficulties?

Ramesh uses his knowledge of his previous interactions with Tom to guide him around exploring his reactions to including cultural competence within their sessions. He uses changes in Tom's body language to enquire about his response to his suggestion and he is then compassionate towards Tom when he became self-critical. Ramesh also admits to his own limitations and then suggests a way forward for the session.

Overcoming barriers to conversations around difference and diversity

Supervisors can be reluctant to raise issues such as difference and diversity due to the fear of offending their supervisee or triggering a rupture. This chapter has provided some examples of how these topics can be raised within supervision to evoke curiosity between the supervision dyad. Occasionally, supervisors may hold inflexible beliefs about the scope of supervision (e.g. 'supervision is only for discussing technical mastery of interventions') which need to be addressed within meta-supervision. Supervisors might wish to set themselves a series of behavioural experiments with predictions about what they believe will happen if they raise issues relating to difference and diversity within supervision sessions.

Questions for meta-supervision

It feels awkward asking about ethnicity or sexuality. What is the most sensitive way of starting a conversation with a supervisee about these aspects of identity?

How will I know if the supervisee has become offended by discussions around difference and diversity?

Chapter summary

- By encouraging supervisees to reflect upon salient aspects of their own identity and how this affects their 'personal self' and 'therapist self', supervisors are showing an openness to exploring cultural factors within supervision and therapy.
- The PSQ can also be introduced within established supervision dyads as part of a scheduled periodic review of learning, goals and the supervisory alliance.
- It is worth noting that simply asking these questions does not mean that the supervisee will feel comfortable expressing all aspects of their identity, especially if they experience shame in relation to this.

- Supervisees could use supervision to rehearse culturally sensitive conversations or explore how their own protected characteristics are magnified within therapy or supervision.
- Supervisors can model 'non-perfection' by sharing their own fear of discussing intersectionality with supervisees or clients.

Recommended reading

Dressel, J. L., Consoli, A. J., Kim, B. S., & Atkinson, D. R. (2007). Successful and unsuccessful multicultural supervisory behaviors: A Delphi poll. *Journal of Multicultural Counseling and Development*, 35(1), 51–64.

Chapter 12

Managing the supervisory relationship

Introduction

Whilst the primary focus of CBT supervision is on promoting learning, we cannot escape from that fact that supervision has the potential to be a hotbed of schema activation for both supervisor and supervisee (Hoffman et al., 2005). For the supervisor, there is often an implicit or at times explicit pressure to 'perform' – to demonstrate one's superior knowledge and skills so as to impress the supervisee or override one's sense of 'imposter syndrome'. This can create anxiety about needing to have all of the answers and can lead to the supervisor working extra hard to show the supervisee that they are worthy of their status. In contrast, for supervisees, supervision is an inherently exposing arena, as they are asked to engage in activities (such as showing videos of their work) that often generate difficult thoughts and feelings. It would seem from the research on these matters that all too often, supervisors and supervisees do not disclose their feelings about each other or the supervisory process (e.g. Yourman, 2003). This suggests that supervisors need to take the lead in providing supervisees with 'checkpoints' where thoughts and feelings can be examined without risk of retribution. This chapter will focus on the use of alliance measures as one means of gauging the effectiveness and safeness of supervision.

The inherent difficulty – safety versus growth

Whilst recognising the importance of supervisee perceptions of safety, supervisors must also hold in mind the primary functions of supervision – to help the supervisee to grow as a therapist. Helping supervisees to grow and develop will inevitably involve some level of discomfort as they try things out in supervision that might lead to them experiencing self-criticism, anxiety, fear, shame and a whole lot more. The CBT supervisor needs to learn when to metaphorically 'put their foot on the accelerator' (e.g. pushing for supervisee growth) and when to 'put their foot on the brake' (e.g. supporting the supervisee and validating where they are at right now). Pushing the supervisee too far or too soon has its problems, yet so does keeping supervision too safe through doing what you have always done in sessions together.

DOI: 10.4324/9781003590620-14

There are three aspects to managing the supervisory relationship (SR) that are addressed in this chapter:

- Agreeing how you will help the supervisee to continue to grow
- Gauging the satisfaction of the supervisee at regular intervals
- Detecting signs of withdrawal or a rupture.

Agreeing how you will help the supervisee to continue to grow

Whilst active methods can be used spontaneously with supervision, it can be helpful to get the supervisee's consent at the start of the relationship about which methods will be used. The Pre-Supervision Questionnaire (PSQ) that was presented in Chapter 10 provides a means of identifying the methods that have been used in previous SR's and the supervisees receptiveness to less familiar methods such as Deliberate Practice (see Chapter 15). Having an explicit agreement in place about what you will do to help the supervisee to answer their supervision questions sets clear expectations as to what will happen in supervision.

Ramesh: I wonder if the best way of answering your question is getting you to play the client and that way, I can show you how I'd elicit that information and then we can swap. How's that sound?

Basma: I'm not sure I feel like doing that today, could we try it next time?

Ramesh: Remember when you completed the PSQ, you identified role-play as something you would try to avoid. I'm wondering if that might be what is happening right now?

Basma: Yeah, I guess so.

Ramesh: What might be the benefits of doing role-play instead of me just giving you advice on this case?

In this vignette, Ramesh does not collude with Basma's urge to avoid role-play and instead, links this behaviour to what had been written in her PSQ. He uses Socratic questioning to help Basma to consider how role-play could be more useful than simply getting his opinion. If Basma continued to resist the idea of role-play, Ramesh has a decision to make in terms of continuing to push for using this method or respecting the wishes of Basma on this occasion.

Gently pushing for active methods

Basma might be happier and have more positive feelings towards Ramesh if he simply agreed with her original intentions of seeking his advice. However, the emotions or reported level of satisfaction of your supervisee are not always the best barometer of the effectiveness of the supervision you are providing. Many supervisees feel understandably anxious about showing recordings or feel uncomfortable doing role-plays; therefore, not having to do this can be negatively reinforcing! Your supervisee might feel happy that they escape the discomfort of their work being scrutinised, but that does not mean this is in their best interests as a therapist. Role-play or watching a recording of their clinical work gives you as supervisor direct access to how they do things rather than just them telling you. This can lead to more targeted feedback and provides opportunities to repeat skills practices that incorporate this.

Supervisor tip: judicious use of self-disclosure

Sharing details of your own anxieties as a therapist or your own thoughts on sharing recordings when you were a trainee can help to normalise the experience of feeling 'under the spotlight'.

Gauging the satisfaction of the supervisee at regular intervals

There are several important reasons to gauge the strength of the SR at regular intervals. Firstly, supervisees can be reluctant to provide honest feedback about what they view as the shortcomings of supervision because of the obvious power differential between supervisor and supervisee. If you simply ask them 'how was today's session?' they might feel obliged to say 'good' or 'okay'. Research suggests that withholding information from supervisors is common (e.g. Mehr et al., 2010) therefore creating more formal channels of communication would seem vital for keeping the SR in good working order.

A supervision experience questionnaire (e.g. the Supervisory Relationship Questionnaire; Palomo et al., 2010), allows for some degree of elaboration on what went well and what not so well. It also communicates to the supervisee that you are receptive to negative feedback (in theory at least!). When considering how to incorporate this into supervision, there are various practical considerations that spring to mind.

How often should they be administered?
Should it be completed during the supervision session or as a homework task?
What is the 'cut-off' score for the supervisor needing to follow this up?
Does the supervisee find it useful?

Reflective exercise

How do you currently gauge the quality of the supervisory relationship with your supervisees?

There are clearly many caveats to how these questions might be answered, however, it goes back to what has been agreed at the start of the SR. Personally, I find a brief measure such as The Leeds Alliance in Supervision Scale (LASS; Wainwright, 2010) more accessible to use session by session. The LASS consists of three items and can be administered relatively quickly at the end of a session (see Figure 12.1).

(Approach)

This supervision session was not focused	⟵ 1 2 3 4 5 6 7 8 9 10 ⟶	This supervision session was focused

(Relationship)

My supervisor and I did not understand each other in this session	⟵ 1 2 3 4 5 6 7 8 9 10 ⟶	My supervisor and I understood each other in this session

(Meeting My Needs)

This supervision session was not helpful to me	⟵ 1 2 3 4 5 6 7 8 9 10 ⟶	This supervision session was helpful to me

Figure 12.1 The Leeds Alliance in Supervision Scale.

Source: Reproduced with permission from N. Wainwright

Supervisor tip

It is a good idea for the supervisor and supervisee to agree on a number on each item or an overall score that would 'flag up' a need for further discussion. For example, a score of lower than 5 on any item within the LASS might point to considerable dissatisfaction with the supervisor's approach, problems within the relationship or the supervisee feeling that their learning needs are not being addressed sufficiently.

Providing feedback to the supervisee

It is equally important for the supervisor to have the opportunity to provide feedback to the supervisee on matters such as their level of skill development but also on their behaviour within supervision. For example, if the supervisor has noticed a pattern of avoidance in relation to bringing video clips, this should be addressed. Likewise, if the supervisor has detected that the supervisee seems to have very prominent negative beliefs about CBT (e.g. Parker & Waller, 2017), it would be useful to bring this up during a review.

Detecting signs of withdrawal or a rupture

The more obvious signs of a rupture might be defensiveness or hostility from a supervisee. Withdrawal can be more subtle, with a gradual change in the number of recordings that are brought or the types of cases or supervision questions. The supervisor can also compare LASS scores over an extended period (e.g. six months) to track what is happening to the ratings.

> Sonia noticed that Trudie was only scoring 6 for each of the three items on the LASS. Whilst they had agreed that a 5 on any item would warrant a follow up email, the change in scores from what they had been previously (8's and 9's) indicated to Sonia that there might be a rupture emerging.

Tips for healing ruptures between supervisee and supervisor

- Try not to take the rupture personally (easier said than done!)
- See the rupture as a process within the relationship which can be observed by both parties with curiosity
- Consider formulating the rupture as a self-supervision exercise prior to discussing with supervisee or take it to SoS.
- Use 'I' statements to discuss feelings and thoughts rather than blaming e.g. 'you make me feel'
- See challenges as an opportunity to strengthen the supervisory relationship

Watch out for your own supervisor avoidance!

Despite one's best efforts, it is not always possible to avert a rupture. Some supervisors might believe that if they avoid certain conversations or activities then a rupture will be prevented. This exposes a belief that ruptures are always a bad thing and that they should be prevented all costs. As with therapist-client relationships, ruptures are inevitable, it is how we respond to them when they occur that is most important (Nelson et al., 2008). The BASS-12 (Appendix 4) can help to identify beliefs that perpetuate avoidance of important conversations about the working alliance in supervision.

Questions for meta-supervision

How often should I administer alliance measures?
What should I do if the supervisee provides negative feedback?

Chapter summary

- Research suggests that supervisees often withhold how they feel in supervision due to feelings of shame, anxiety and the power differential.
- CBT Supervisors may also withhold negative feelings (e.g. frustration) that they experience towards their supervisees.
- Supervisees who feel safe are more likely to disclose, therefore it is a good idea to gauge the strength of the alliance periodically using a scale such as the LASS.
- Failing to address the cognitions and emotions of supervisees may drive the urge to hide aspects of their work from the supervisor, meaning that opportunities for skill development are missed.
- The emotions or reported level of satisfaction of your supervisee are not always the best barometer of the effectiveness of the supervision you are providing. Similarly, a failure to elicit feedback on supervisee satisfaction may increase the risk of supervision-interfering behaviours.
- Having regular conversations around the agreed goals and tasks of supervision and gauging the strength of the bond, could potentially avert a rupture at a later stage.

Recommended reading

Mehr, K. E., Ladany, N., & Caskie, G. I. (2010). Trainee nondisclosure in supervision: What are they not telling you? *Counselling and Psychotherapy Research*, 10(2), 103–113.

Part III

How to get more active in supervision

Chapter 13

Using routine outcome measures to guide clinical decision making

Introduction

Where Part II gave some ideas around how to create solid foundations within supervision, Part III provides examples of specific activities that can support supervisee learning across supervision sessions. Routine outcome monitoring (ROM) as it is commonly referred to, helps the supervisee to consider if what they are doing in therapy is having a tangible effect on the client's presenting problems. ROM usually consists of three elements (Barkham et al., 2023):

1 Collecting scores on a regular basis
2 Providing feedback on the patterns in these scores week by week (or every session)
3 Adapting treatment based on these patterns

In the UK, the development of the Improving Access To Psychological Therapies (IAPT) programme led to a more target-based approach to therapy (Clark, 2011). In keeping with this, supervision structures became focused on details such as session numbers, changes in scores on a specific range of psychometric measures and client throughput (Harper et al., 2020). Pugh and Margetts (2020) identified the absence or deprioritising of outcome monitoring as one of the main indicators for supervisory drift, therefore this chapter considers some of ways in which ROM can support the aims of CBT supervision, whilst addressing some of the challenges that can arise from the use of ROM.

Supervisor tip

Anecdotal experience suggests that the emphasis on ROM within CBT seems to polarise clinicians, with one camp viewing it as a helpful and necessary means of monitoring the effectiveness of treatment and the other viewing it as a time-consuming or punitive tool that blames therapists for clients not recovering within a set period of time (Roscoe, 2021d; Rye et al., 2019).

DOI: 10.4324/9781003590620-16

The pros and cons of ROM

Through a reductionistic lens, ROM has become a simplistic way of determining whether or not a therapist is competent, with those achieving higher 'recovery rates' deemed to be more competent and therefore 'better' therapists (Rizq, 2012). Applying this definition, recovery occurs when a score on an arbitrary psychometric scale falls below a certain threshold. Measures such as the Patient Health Questionnaire (PHQ-9; Kroenke et al., 2001) and Generalised Anxiety Disorder (GAD-7; Spitzer et al., 1999) are often used to justify access to services but also, an individual's scores can suggest when treatment has done what it set out to, or if it is not having the desired effect (Wade & Waller, 2025). This approach has attracted many critics (e.g. Bruun, 2023) and in truth, there are many flaws that are inherent in solely basing clinical decisions on ROMS (e.g. the client rates their distress lower to appease the therapist, or the scale measures the reduction of something that is not fully describing the subjective experience of the client).

In healthcare systems like the NHS that rely on 'proving their worth' to policymakers, ROMS play an essential role in securing funding, whilst in contexts such as private practice they retain a pragmatic value. On the positive side, clients can find it reassuring that others experience similar thoughts and engage in similar behaviours when reading the items on these questionnaires (e.g. Purdon & Clark, 1993). ROM can also address 'all or nothing' thinking about progress (e.g. 'nothing has changed versus 'I'm completely better') by helping clients to see incremental improvements. It can also help therapists to re-evaluate their formulation or interventions by considering the impact that these have had on presenting symptoms.

Perhaps the most compelling reason for using ROMs is their capacity to improve therapy outcomes. For example, Delgadillo et al. (2022) found that their use narrowed the gap between higher and lower performing therapists. In summary, ROMS have their place in monitoring therapy outcomes and are one of several tools that can support the focus of supervision. Some supervisees may have negative attitudes towards the use of ROMS, or, in contrast, place too much emphasis on ROMS, by overlooking other markers of client improvement.

> **Reflective exercise**
>
> What is your attitude towards ROM?
> How often do you include this within supervision sessions?

ROM informed supervision

The next part of this chapter will consider how ROM can inform our work as supervisors (see Swift et al., 2015), by using them as a basis for understanding the supervisee's current level of knowledge and skills. We can then segue into other active supervision methods such as role-playing how to review ROMS or exploring therapist blocks (e.g. negative attitudes to using them with clients).

Noticing patterns in clinical outcomes

ROM can help to steer supervisors towards understanding patterns in areas where supervisees excel or struggle. For example, a supervisor may observe that a supervisee generally gets good outcomes when working with anxiety disorders yet not so good outcomes when the client has depression.

> Ramesh asked Basma to bring session by session ROMs to their supervision so that they could track the effects that specific interventions seemed to be having on the client's presenting problems. Despite Basma reporting that treatment was going well, when they looked at the trend over the first eight sessions, they could see that the client's scores were not reducing significantly. This helped to focus the direction of supervision and to revise the formulation and treatment plan.

Establishing how the supervisee introduces and uses ROM across a course of therapy

It can be helpful to discuss the supervisees current use of ROM during the contracting phase. For example, as a supervisor you might ask

Which measures do you use or not use? What are your reasons for this?
How often do you administer them? What are your reasons for this?

Exploring moderating factors

Contextual factors will play a part in how supervisees respond to these questions. For example, in NHS settings, session by session ROMs are often mandated, therefore if the supervisee is not adhering to this, there is a need for the supervisor to address this with the aim of supporting the supervisee to comply with service policies. In PP depending on the referral source (e.g. self-funding clients) there is more freedom for therapists to choose how they use outcome measures. Furthermore, when the supervisee has selected their supervisor like many do in PP, the power dynamic is more even. The supervisee in this context, may choose to dispense with the services of a supervisor if they insist on implementing ROM in a manner that does not fit with their preferred way of working. This is not to say that supervisees in PP can and should do what they want, and that the supervisor should be permissive; it is merely a point that they have less 'role power' than NHS counterparts (Holloway, 1995)

Selecting the most appropriate self-report measures

There are occasions where the supervisor can guide their supervisee towards using measures that have greater specificity in relation to their presenting problems. Alternatively, supervisors can recommend additional questionnaires that identify transdiagnostic (e.g. dysfunctional attitudes; Weissman & Beck, 1978) or disorder-specific factors (e.g. the Obsessive Compulsive Inventory (OCI); Foa et al., 1998).

> Sonny was familiar with the PHQ-9 and GAD-7, giving these to all of his clients however, he had not heard of some of the disorder-specific measures that track symptoms more specific to the presenting problem. Sonia suggested that he also use the OCI as this would identify symptoms more specific to the problems his client was reporting.
>
> Tom was working with a client whose PHQ-9 and GAD-7 scores were below the recognised threshold at intake and after several assessment sessions. Sonia suggested that he use a measure that was more sensitive to his client's presenting problems (Perfectionism) to track progress over the course of treatment.

Barriers to the use of ROM

The final part of this chapter considers some of the barriers to the use of ROMS that might need to be addressed within supervision. Broadly speaking we can view these as either therapist/supervisor-related, client-related or contextual factors that interfere with ROM.

Supervisor and supervisee beliefs

Research suggests that many therapists overestimate their effectiveness (e.g. view their work through 'rose tinted glasses') meaning that subjective report of improvement should be treated with caution (Brosan et al., 2008). This can lead to therapists either disregarding questionnaire scores (e.g. 'my perception of the client's progress tells me more than a change in their score can' or administering them infrequently (e.g. 'I will know when it is worthwhile checking the score again'). Furthermore, supervisors can be susceptible to the 'halo effect' (Thorndike, 1920) whereby they only see their supervisees positive qualities due to their personal characteristics (e.g. likeability) or level of clinical experience.

There are also therapists that outright reject the usefulness of ROM because they associate it with classifications of mental illness that are incompatible with how they view the world (Lee et al., 2013). Some therapists also believe that ROM does not capture information that is truly significant to them or their clients.

> Both Sonia and Sonny held negative beliefs about the usefulness of ROM for determining whether or not a client was suffering from a particular disorder or if they were improving from treatment. Sonia took this issue to meta-supervision

to consider how there was the risk of collusion with Sonny to discount the information from ROM or to omit them completely.

Client factors

It is important to consider how the supervisee is administering ROMs and the challenges that go with this. For example, some will use paper copies, whilst others will email them to clients to complete and send ahead of the session. Some clients will have difficulties reading and writing whilst others might struggle to access certain forms of technology. There are also clients who view ROM as time consuming and irrelevant to them or who rate their scores the same at every session despite other indicators of improvement.

Contextual factors

In terms of being able to analyse changes in scores, therapists in PP are unlikely to have access to sophisticated ROM systems (ad described in Delgadillo et al., 2022) that provides alerts based on observable trends. In the absence of this, an Excel spreadsheet or graph paper can provide at least some means of tracking scores. Supervisors should encourage supervisees to bring the overview of scores to supervision in whichever format they use.

A sensible way forward?

Having explained the potential value of ROM, there is also the risk that some therapists and supervisors, place too much importance on scores to determine diagnoses, overlooking other stressors (e.g. socioeconomic factors) thus leading to premature discharges of clients or unnecessary questioning of therapist competence if scores do not fit with overall service 'trends'. In 2021, I wrote an article about uncoupling your worth as a therapist from ROM scores (see Roscoe, 2021d). This was based on my observations that many therapists are quick to compare themselves negatively with others based on recovery rates alone. Supervisors should therefore be vigilant for signs of self-criticism amongst their supervisees which could be an early warning sign of impending burnout.

Questions for meta-supervision

My supervisee has very negative attitudes towards ROMS, what is the best way of addressing this with them?

My own use of ROMS is inconsistent, am I being a hypocrite by asking my supervisees to use them?

Chapter summary

- When 'held lightly', questionnaires help therapist and client to track the progress of treatment and to evaluate the impact of various interventions on a session-by-session basis.
- It is important to enquire about the value that each supervisee places on ROM and to consider the degree to which this aligns with your own views. A rejection of ROM can be indicative of more pervasive negatives attitudes towards CBT.
- If you have negative views about their value, there is the risk that you might collude with a supervisee to avoid or underemphasise this role in reviewing treatment.
- If you place considerable importance on ROM, consider how this influences the feedback you provide to your supervisees.

Recommended reading

Swift, J. K., Callahan, J. L., Rousmaniere, T. G., Whipple, J. L., Dexter, K., & Wrape, E. R. (2015). Using client outcome monitoring as a tool for supervision. *Psychotherapy*, 52(2), 180.

Chapter 14

Reviewing live material

Introduction

Live supervision by definition, consists of the supervisor having access to video or audio recordings of a supervisee's work, or sitting in and observing a live therapy session (BABCP, 2025; Weck et al., 2016). It is a fundamental component of effective supervision regardless of the supervisee's level of experience (Stoltenberg & McNeill, 2010). It is often mandated during CBT training, where supervisors are required to view a specific number of sessions before the supervisee can pass their course. Conversely, it is all too common for supervisors to stop asking to see samples of the supervisee's work once they are qualified (see Townend et al., 2002) despite it being a requirement for continued accreditation with the main CBT body (BABCP). It is worthwhile reflecting on your own attitudes towards reviewing live material before reading the rest of this chapter, as this is likely to determine the degree to which you incorporate this method within supervision.

Reflective exercise

Thinking about your own clinical practice, how often do you bring recordings of your therapy sessions to your own supervisor? What are the factors that determine the frequency in which this is undertaken?

How does your own use of video feedback influence your behaviour towards your supervisees in this respect?

Why we need to keep live material on the supervision agenda

I will argue that omitting live material is shortsighted on a number of levels (see Gonsalvez et al., 2016) therefore, the aim of this chapter is to underscore the reasons why reviewing live material is crucial across the career span.

DOI: 10.4324/9781003590620-17

Over-estimation of competence

Studies have shown that therapists tend to over-estimate their competence (e.g. Brosan et al., 2008) suggesting that relying on self-report from supervisees could be an unwise decision. A vicious cycle can develop as a result of the supervisee failing to receive correct feedback on their actual rather than perceived therapeutic skills. Figure 14.1 shows how over-estimating one's competence can lead to deprioritising video feedback and in doing so, the supervisee misses out on opportunities to improve their skills.

A similar cycle could be drawn out for supervisees who underestimate their competence and avoid bringing clips of their clinical work due to fears of being criticised or 'found out' to be the imposter they believe themselves to be.

Tracking skill development

The Declarative Procedural Reflective (DPR) model (Bennett-Levy, 2006) and the Integrative Developmental Model (IDM; Stoltenberg, 1981) that were summarised in Chapters 5 and 6, provide CBT supervisors with two very robust frameworks for tracking supervisee skill development across several domains. In terms of the DPR model, case discussion alone can be difficult for judging the supervisee's procedural skills. It is possible that a supervisee might grasp the theory (e.g. declarative knowledge) but struggle to put it into action, therefore being able to view what they do and how they do it is crucial in gauging clinical competence. For example, seeing how they interact with clients is also a window into their interpersonal skills, as some CBT therapists will be competent in developing a formulation or

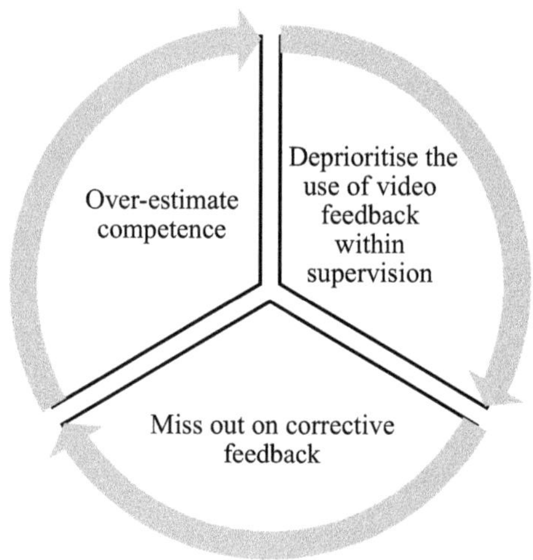

Figure 14.1 The relationship between over-estimation of competence and underutilisation of video feedback.

undertaking and intervention, however, they might do so with insufficient empathy or validation.

If we consider the IDM, qualified therapists or more experienced trainees can get 'stuck' developmentally in various domains. For example, some later stage trainees will be at Level 2 whilst others will still be at Level 1. An over-reliance on case discussion means that the supervisee effectively 'filters' the information that is available to the supervisor, meaning that key aspects of skill development can remain 'out of sight'.

> In comparison to some of his fellow trainees, Tom had remained at Level 1 in several IDM domains, specifically case conceptualisation and interpersonal skills. Ramesh had noticed that Tom continued to rely on basic 5 areas formulations rather than adopting the disorder-specific alternatives. When discussing his cases, Tom would usually bypass what formulation he had used, and it would have been difficult to assess how he was interacting with his clients without video review. Watching clips of his clinical work showed that Tom continued to behave in quite a 'teacher-like' manner towards his clients, rather than adopting a more Socratic approach. Viewing video recordings were essential in helping Ramesh to observe this.

Ramesh was able to use these observations to plan the use of other active methods that could support Tom in these areas. For example, modelling Socratic Dialogue within supervision and asking Tom to have a go at drawing out disorder-specific formulations are methods that can be interspersed with video feedback.

> Having drawn out a Panic model in supervision, Tom agreed to record his next therapy session where he would do with his client. This helped Ramesh to gauge Tom's declarative knowledge of Panic Disorder in action, as well as his competence in mapping out the maintenance cycle. Ramesh could then revisit any misunderstandings or residual deficits in procedural skill.

Stoltenberg and McNeill (2010) also talk about 'pseudo-level 3' therapists who might be able to 'talk a good game' but their clinical skills do not match up with their level of experience. These are likely to be qualified therapists rather than trainees who have had little exposure to certain types of presentations (e.g. PTSD) or have actively avoided working with them. Some supervisees can become very adept at avoiding bringing live material and therefore sooner or later, the supervisor is encouraged to raise this with them.

> Trudie would often talk at length about her understanding of complex trauma, however, she gave minimal evidence of having a thorough understanding of how to work with PTSD using evidence-based CBT models. Trudie would often state that her clients were unwilling to be recorded. Eventually, Trudie had to bring a recording as part of maintaining her accreditation and viewing this recording of her work with a PTSD client helped Sonia to see that there was very poor model fidelity on show.

Using competence measures to support video feedback

The Cognitive Therapy Scale Revised (CTS-R; Blackburn et al., 2001) is perhaps the most commonly used generic competence measure within CBT training and supervision, certainly within a UK context. Supervisors might view a full session or more commonly, a 5–10 minute clip, whilst considering one or two items (e.g. collaboration, feedback). In addition to showing adherence to generic CBT principles (e.g. the presence of an agenda, guided discovery and homework), the supervisor is looking for signs of competence in the application of specific 'change methods' that fit with the existing formulation. Scales have been developed to measure the disorder-specific competences when treating problems such as OCD (see Bream et al., 2017) and there are also scales that can closely examine specific universal competences such as homework setting (e.g. The Homework Adherence and Competence Scale (HAAC); Wedge, 2005). Combining these scales with reviewing a video or audio recording, helps supervisors to provide more targeted feedback than would be possible from simply discussing the content of a therapy session (Gonsalvez et al., 2016).

> Basma had not been aware of how quickly she was speaking during a therapy session and reflected after watching a recording that she needed to address her pacing and use of feedback.
>
> When considering interpersonal effectiveness, Sonny reflected that his body language and facial expression appeared more 'cold and shut off' from his client than he had believed at the time.

Whilst qualified therapists no longer need to 'pass' a CTS-R to maintain their accreditation, adhering to the overall principles that are captured in this measure, is likely to be key to enduring fidelity to the generic cognitive model. It is important to move beyond the tokenism of bringing one video a year to 'tick a box'. Instead, supervisors can help their supervisees to see the value in career long video feedback.

> Trudie was initially defensive when Sonia suggested that she bring videos of her work with PTSD clients to supervision. As a means of trying to remove the shame that could be associated with this, Sonia shared her own struggles with understanding some models and treatment protocols post-qualification. Once they reviewed a recording, Trudie admitted that she found some aspects of the Ehlers and Clark (200) model difficult to understand but felt embarrassed given that she was qualified. Hearing Sonia's experiences normalised her difficulties.

Live supervision as a gateway to other active methods

As Trudie's experience shows, live supervision is often essential in pinpointing areas of skill development that require attention. It also highlights how we as supervisors might wrongly assume competence just because someone has passed a training course. Furthermore, supervisees can hold problematic rules and assumptions about what they 'should' or should not' know by a certain stage or be able to do.

Having agreed a skill domain to focus on, the video or audio clip can be seen as a gateway into using other active methods. For example, watching or hearing parts of a therapy session can lead to a follow up exercise such as the supervisor demonstrating how they deliver the intervention with the client, as a means of comparison. This could be done purely as a way of modelling a technique or formulation, or the scenario could be 'reenacted' with the supervisee playing the client to get a sense of what it is like to be on the receiving end of both 'styles' of therapy. This could then lead to a swapping of role, whereby the supervisee plays the role of therapist, replicating the actions of the supervisor.

> Sonia asked Trudie if she would find it helpful for them to role-play the clinical scenario within the video clip. Firstly, Sonia asked Trudie to play the client as she replicated what Trudie said and did during the clip. Sonia then asked Trudie to reflect on what it was like to be the client.

Identifying and managing obstacles to live supervision

There can be a range of obstacles that supervisor and supervisee need to overcome when factoring live elements into supervision sessions. Being able to sit in on your supervisee's live session can be a challenge for several reasons including how acceptable it is to clients, co-ordinating diaries and room space. Then, there is the time required to go over the supervisor's feedback. Online working has made this potentially easier and there are more novel methods such as 'Bug in the eye' (BITE) supervision whereby visual prompts are provided to the supervisee in the session (see Weck et al., 2016).

Reviewing video or audio clips involves some degree of preparation in terms of reviewing the recording ahead of the session to select the part that will be shown, however, it is often the beliefs of the supervisor or supervisee that interfere with live supervision.

Supervisor tip

In the same way that supervisees can hold problematic assumptions, unhelpful supervisor assumptions can contribute towards the avoidance or under-emphasise of live supervision. Several items on the BASS-12 (see Appendix 4) can help to identify beliefs which may interfere with the use of regular live material. Some of the beliefs that supervisors and supervisees may hold about reviewing live material are described below.

It is too time consuming

An obvious disadvantage to reviewing therapy recordings within supervision is that it can be time consuming, especially if the supervisee wants to discuss several cases during that meeting. Setting a realistic agenda that takes account of the supervisees wishes but also the supervisors duties (e.g. normative oversight) is key here. There are also a couple of techniques (e.g. Give me 5 and I-spy*)* that can be used to summarise the feedback and to make it a more collaborative undertaking (see Gonsalvez et al., 2016). BITE supervision as described by Weck et al. (2016) has the advantage of taking place 'there and then' but many services might face challenges with implementing this (e.g. funds for technology; client consent).

It is not necessary to formally rate the skills of qualified supervisees

This belief indicates a faulty assumption that all skills are acquired within training and is jumping to the conclusion that supervisees will not find this beneficial. As discussed earlier in the chapter, video feedback can be modified by using more bespoke competence measures or by making it more collaborative, so it feels less like a formal evaluation and more like a valued learning exercise.

It would be terrible to experience a rupture within supervision

Supervisees can be highly avoidant of bringing recordings to supervision and there comes a time where supervisors need to empathically confront the supervisee with the necessity of this and the consequences of continuing to avoid. Supervisors who view their supervisees as too emotionally fragile, or the supervisory relationship as liable to break any time they suggest a challenging exercise, might be tempted to avoid this task. This can be unhelpful for several reasons. Firstly, whilst avoiding asking supervisees to bring live material may prevent awkward conversations, especially if they are qualified, the long-term consequence is that you remain relatively 'in the dark' about their actual skills and are reliant on self-report. The other major consequence is that the supervisee is missing out on valuable feedback to correct gaps in declarative knowledge (e.g. misunderstandings) or to improve procedural skills (e.g. Murray et al., 2022). There are of course parallels that the supervisor can draw with how the supervisee behaves with their client. Asking the supervisee to consider how they would deal with an avoidant client could help them to apply some CBT principles to themselves (Bennett-Levy, 2019).

Reflective exercise

Complete the BASS-12 (Appendix 4).
Were there any items that you endorsed?

Where have these beliefs come from?
How do these beliefs affect how you behave towards trainees, qualified therapists or both?
What could be the unintended consequences of holding these beliefs?

In addition to answering the questions within the BASS-12, supervisors might find it useful to complete the Therapist Schema Questionnaire (Leahy, 2001) to identify specific schemas that could make them more likely to avoid asking supervisees to bring recordings. For example, 'Need for approval' and 'Self-Sacrifice' are two of the most common therapist schemas (Haarhoff, 2006) and their presence is likely to mean that supervisors will do almost anything to please their supervisee, including neglecting their normative duties.

Questions for meta-supervision

How can I encourage qualified supervisees to continue to bring recordings to supervision?
How should I manage persistent supervisee avoidance or defensiveness when asked to share recordings of this clinical work?

Chapter summary

- Research suggests that a significant amount of therapists over-estimate their clinical competence, meaning that reliance on self-report is fraught with difficulties.
- Reviewing live material remains an important task for qualified supervisees.
- Video or audio feedback can be combined or followed up with other active methods.
- Your own beliefs about showing recordings might interfere with setting limits on supervisee avoidance.

Recommended reading

Gonsalvez, C. J., Brockman, R., & Hill, H. R. (2016). Video feedback in CBT supervision: Review and illustration of two specific techniques. *The Cognitive Behaviour Therapist*, 9, e24.

Chapter 15

Scaffolding therapists learning through Deliberate Practice

Introduction

Deliberate Practice (DP) is a way of developing competence in a specific skill and has been applied across many disciplines including sport, medicine, chess and psychotherapy (Mahon, 2023). Unlike other training methods such as role- plays, Observed Structured Clinical Examinations (OSCEs), anecdotal experience suggests that DP has not been widely adopted within UK CBT training courses. There is, however, a CBT manual that has been written to support the use of DP (see Boswell & Constantino, 2021) and various journal papers have been published that highlight the value of this training method (e.g. Mahon, 2023; McLeod, 2022). The aim of this chapter is to explain how DP can be used by CBT supervisors to help therapists at all stages of their career to become more proficient in the use of specific CBT methods.

DP in a nutshell

DP was developed by Anders Ericsson (see Ericsson et al., 1993) as a framework for understanding how individuals learn to excel in any given field. Clements-Hickman and Harris (2024) neatly summarise DP as consisting of 'practice activities designed by a teacher or coach to move performers beyond current levels of performance via intense engagement and immediate feedback' (p564). For example, a tennis player might practice the same shot (e.g. a slice) over and over as a specific training strategy, if this has been a weakness in competitions. In psychotherapy, techniques or formulations where the supervisee lacks confidence or competence are ideal to focus on with DP (McLeod, 2022). DP is different from other active methods such as role-play which might take place during a lecture, or OSCEs in that it involves repeating a skill numerous times in quick succession, implementing live feedback each time.

Advantages of DP

Given that CBT training courses are relatively short in duration (e.g. usually one year) and that a skill might be role-played only once in a teaching session, DP could

DOI: 10.4324/9781003590620-18

provide considerable value if it was incorporated within supervision. For example, being able to practice explaining the Clark (1986) Panic model three times in succession, allows the supervisee to quickly implement changes following feedback from their supervisor each time. In a standard role-play format, it might be more difficult to establish if changes have been adopted by the supervisee as the demonstration of the skill is not repeated.

Selecting a skill for DP

The work of Lev Vygotsky is relevant to the underpinnings of DP in that the aim is to help the supervisee to expand their zone of proximal development (ZPD; Vygotsky, 1978). Sacks and Vaz (2023) describe the ZPD as 'the sweet-spot between practice that is too easy to make a difference and tasks that are too hard to handle' (p261). Feedback from Cognitive Therapy Scale Revised (CTS-R; Blackburn et al., 2001) marking sheets can help trainees to pinpoint specific skills to work on during DP (e.g. agenda setting). There might also be a specific technique that one has not had the opportunity to use in clinical practice. For example, role-playing a worry script in a teaching session in March means that skills are prone to decay if the supervisee does not take on use this with any clients until November.

Getting started with DP

DP can be delivered within one-to-one supervision or within a group format. In this chapter, an example is provided for use within the first scenario. The steps that are involved during DP (based on McLeod, 2022) are outlined below.

- Choose a specific intervention or formulation to work on
- Agree on what competence would look like in the role-play (e.g. using CTS-R criterion descriptions for a scoring between 0–6)
- Choose your level of difficulty: 'Easy', 'moderately challenging' or 'Difficult'
- If you are doing this within a group, you can ask each supervisee to take it in turns to be therapist, client and observer
- Client and observer(s) will provide immediate verbal feedback
- Therapist then repeats the intervention using feedback (either as an 'easy' case or, moving up to 'moderately challenging')
- In a group context, repeat until each member of the group has had one turn as therapist and/or been able to repeat their intervention following receipt of feedback

DP example – interoceptive exposure (symptom induction)

Whilst Sonny understood the theory of how to treat Panic Disorder, he struggled to know how to put this into action when working with clients, especially those who expressed reluctance to take part in the interoceptive exposure tasks. Sonia suggested that they use DP as a way of him gaining more confidence. Sonny had never heard of this training method before but agreed to give it a go. Together, they agreed what would be an 'easy', 'moderately challenging' or 'difficult' version of this intervention.

Easy – take the client through a hyperventilation experiment where the person playing the client does not become overly distressed.
Moderately challenging – the client expresses some reluctance or scepticism about undertaking the experiment
Difficult – client expresses considerable reluctance, then become distressed during the experiment

Sonny felt confident in using the hyperventilation experiment with 'easy' clients, so he chose a scenario whereby Sonia played a slightly avoidant and sceptical client. After Sonny's first attempt at doing this, Sonia provided immediate verbal feedback.

Sonia: How do you feel that went then Sonny?
Sonny: Not great, I really struggled when you said it didn't feel anything like a real panic attack.
Sonia: Ok, and what did you do in response to my behaviour that you think you could improve upon?
Sonny: I think I was trying to convince you rather than treating it as an experiment.
Sonia: Good reflection there. Yes, I agree, I think you were desperate to get me to do the experiment and in doing so, you didn't allow enough time to explore my concerns. Should we try it again and this time, try to use guided discovery to understand my concerns and propose that we treat it as an experiment.

Sonny repeated the role-play, with amendments. After the second 'round' of DP, Sonia again provided feedback. Due to time constraints, they did not do a third round. Sonny reflected that he had gained more confidence in dealing with clients who are unsure about whether to engage in symptom induction for Panic.

Reflective exercise

Think of a current supervisee and one of their main areas for skill development How might you use Deliberate Practice to support them instead of your usual 'go to' methods?

Practical considerations

The length of the supervision session, the number of group members and the skill that has been selected will determine the number of times one can repeat the skill. For example, Sonia could plan a longer than usual supervision session with Sonny (e.g. 90 minutes rather than 60) to fit in more rounds of DP. This will depend on service policies and constraints (e.g. supervisor and supervisee caseloads) therefore, not everyone will have this luxury.

Reporting on a pilot of DP within a psychotherapy training programme, McLeod (2022) found that 30 minutes was the most frequently recorded time that trainees allocated to this, however many of the respondents were engaged in self-directed DP rather than using it within supervision.

Gauging supervisee reactions to DP

As with any supervision method, it is important to gain informed consent from the supervisee. For example:

Do they understand the rationale for why they are doing it?
Do they have any concerns, if so, what are they?

Some level of trepidation is to be expected as they are demonstrating their skills in front of someone that are likely to be inferior to or in competition with. A helpful stance is to strongly encourage, reaffirming the potential benefits to them whilst respecting their right to decline on that occasion.

> **Supervisor tip**
>
> As with any experiential method, there is the chance that some supervisees will express reluctance to take part. Including DP within the discussions during contracting will help to make it less of a surprise when it is suggested within a supervision session. Qualified therapists might bauk at the idea of DP if they are defensive about their skill level or perceive it to be a task that is only for novices.

Monitoring for signs of self-criticism and shame

For the supervisees that do take part in DP, the process might trigger self-criticism if they perceive that they have underperformed. This might be failing to live up to their own standards or focusing in on the negative aspects of feedback from their supervisor. It is important that supervisors normalise the need to repeat role-plays rather than expecting to get it perfect first time.

Monitoring for subtle levels of avoidance and the use of safety behaviours

As discussed in Chapter 8, therapists will use safety behaviours as a way of managing feelings of anxiety, fear and shame. Within DP this could manifest as trying to talk about the exercise (e.g. intellectualising) rather than immersing themselves in the task. Others might use humour as a way of making it feel less like an evaluation, therefore it is important for the supervisor to consider the function of any behaviour that seems to detract from the supervisee being fully focused.

Potential challenges

Clements-Hickman and Harris (2024) raises important questions that must be addressed, such as

Who is expert enough to give the feedback?
How is success measured?
Which activities count as DP task?

At this point in time, there seems to be a lack of clarity of what is and is not DP. For example, McLeod (2022) reported that some of the activities recorded on students DP logs seemed more like self-practice (e.g. watching YouTube demonstrations).

It is also worth considering that many CBT supervisors will be unfamiliar with DP given that it is not embedded within training curriculums. On this basis, it is sensible to obtain a copy of the training manual (Boswell & Constantino, 2021) or to try out their own DP before implementing this with their supervisees.

Linking DP with other active methods

DP is highly compatible with other active methods, such as video feedback, supervisor modelling and chair work. For example, having shown a video in supervision, the supervisor could suggest DP as a way of implementing the feedback on what they have seen in the recording. Conversely, the supervisor might suggest that as 'homework' the supervisee record a session of them putting into practice what they did in DP and bring it to the next session to review how these changes went. The supervisor might wish to model the skill that will be the focus of DP, or if the supervisee expresses reluctance to take part, they could use chair work to 'speak to' the part of them that wants to avoid the task, to better understand these barriers (see Roscoe, 2021b). Lastly, skill rehearsal could segue into Self-Practice/Self-Reflection (SP/SR) if the supervisee is struggling to know how to deliver the intervention in a way that feel personable, or if they have lived experience of a particular mental health problem, SP/SR might help them to reflect on barriers to engaging in specific CBT tasks (Bennett-Levy, 2019).

Questions for meta-supervision

Can we try out DP as I'm not sure I feel confident enough to use it with my supervisees?
How can we fit DP into the supervisee's already packed agenda?

Chapter summary

- DP involves targeted, repetitive practice supported by a tutor or supervisor, with real-time feedback.
- Unlike role-plays or OSCEs, DP focuses on repeated execution and refinement of a skill in quick succession.
- DP allows for a rapid implementation of feedback (e.g. practicing Clark's Panic model multiple times in one supervision session).
- Supervisors may need training or personal experience with using DP before they feel confident enough to incorporate it within supervision sessions.

Recommended reading

Clements-Hickman, A. L., & Reese, R. J. (2020). Improving therapists' effectiveness: Can deliberate practice help? *Professional Psychology: Research and Practice*, 51(6), 606.

Chapter 16

Self-practice of CBT methods

Introduction

Practicing specific CBT techniques in the form of role- plays is a well-established component of CBT training, with courses often required to divide teaching material evenly between theory and practice (e.g. BABCP, 2025). In contrast to role-play, where trainees usually rehearse techniques based on fictional vignettes, working with real difficulties ('real play') offers another dimension of learning. Whilst using personal material poses various challenges within training (e.g. selecting experiences that are not 'too hot' or too cold' emotionally) it provides trainees with the opportunity to see how CBT methods work 'in real life' (Freeston et al., 2019). Formally reflecting on these experiences (an approach known as Self-Practice/Self-Reflection) has been shown to have a range of additional benefits for trainee and experienced therapists (Bennett-Levy, 2019). For example, outcome studies show that both trainee and qualified therapists report enhanced technical and interpersonal skills as a result of engaging in SP/SR (e.g. Davis et al., 2015) as well as having more empathy for their clients. Unlike some other therapeutic modalities, CBT does not mandate personal therapy for trainees, therefore, in the absence of these formal experiences of being 'in the client's chair', SP/SR helps to deepen CBT therapists understanding of the model and methods 'from the inside out' (Bennett-Levy et al., 2001, 2014).

The role of self-practice in therapist skill development

This chapter will provide an overview of how formal self-practice such as SP/SR and more informal methods (e.g. tracking therapist schemas) can be incorporated within supervision. SP/SR (and other forms of personal practice) is thought to create a 'reflective bridge' between the 'personal self' and 'therapist self' (Bennett-Levy, 2019) therefore supervisors may find themselves working with one or both of these 'selves' within supervision.

SP/SR has traditionally been run as an adjunct to CBT training rather than a core component of the teaching curriculum (Freeston et al., 2019) with anecdotal experience suggesting that there is huge variance in the appetite and enthusiasm for SP/SR amongst CBT tutors. Furthermore, many therapists have never heard of

DOI: 10.4324/9781003590620-19

it, despite it being developed over twenty years ago (Bennett-Levy et al., 2001). Readers who are completely unfamiliar with SP/SR are encouraged to access more detailed publications on the approach to therapist skill development.

Integrating SP/SR within supervision

The contracting stage of supervision allows the supervisor to explore the supervisee's receptiveness to active methods such as SP/SR. If the supervisee is unfamiliar with this approach then the supervisor can provide a brief rationale and invite them to consider including it within supervision.

> **Supervisor tip**
>
> It should be stated to every supervisee that self-practice is an unconditional part of supervision. The difference here is the addition of the 'self-reflection' component. The supervision dyad should consider how this is done in a way that is structured and meaningful.

Linking SP/SR to clinical and supervision related challenges

Rather than setting arbitrary SP/SR tasks for supervisees, it makes most sense to suggest this activity in relation to a specific clinical challenge (e.g. behaving in a self-sacrificing way with a client) or a supervision-interfering behaviour (e.g. repeatedly avoiding showing videos). In their paper on active methods and supervisory drift, Pugh and Margetts (2020) include a helpful table with examples of problematic therapist beliefs which can be targeted through the use of behavioural experiments within supervision or as a 'homework' task.

> When reviewing an OCD case that Trudie was treating, it became apparent that she had avoided modelling a Thought-Action Fusion (TAF) experiment for her client and had introduced the intervention in an overly cautious way. Sonia used a combination of macro and micro-skills to address this therapy-interfering behaviour. Firstly, Sonia encouraged Trudie to engage in self-practice within the supervision session (doing the TAF experiment).
>
> Sonia suggested that they both write down the name of a loved one and then asked Trudie to write that she would receive a phone call in the next five minutes to inform her that her loved one had died in an accident. After five minutes had elapsed with no phone call received, Sonia asked Trudie if this was something she would have been able to do with her client. Trudie reflected that she had needed some evidence for 'Theory B' before feeling confident to try this in clinic.
>
> Trudie also completed the Negative Attitudes towards CBT Scale (Parker & Waller, 2017) to help identify specific cognitions that might show up in other

cases in the future. Beyond this, Sonia could also map out the reciprocal processes of how her own anxiety was giving her client the message that her intrusions were dangerous. The cognitive interpersonal cycle formulation (Moorey, 2013) is particularly useful in these instances.

In contrast to Trudie, who held concerns about the implications of using certain CBT interventions, other therapists might struggle with the style and structure of CBT.

Despite knowing how to set an agenda and review homework, Tom would often acquiesce to the emotional content that his clients brought to each session, believing it to be invalidating to implement structure or to stipulate what is and is not to be discussed each time.

Tom would also try to debate with his supervisor Ramesh about the merits of other therapeutic approaches, detracting from time being focused on addressing his actual supervision questions. Rather than getting drawn into a debate or trying to persuade Tom that an agenda would not be invalidating, Ramesh suggested that they investigate this using a behavioural experiment (BE; see Figure 16.1)

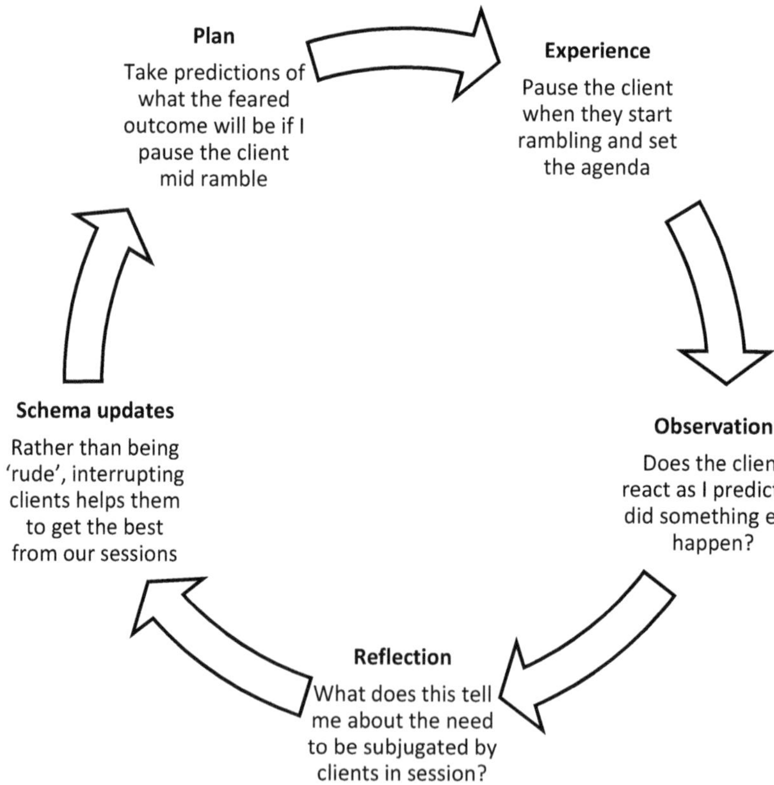

Figure 16.1 Outcome of therapist behavioural experiment.

Table 16.1 Self practice/self-reflection reflection form

What was your experience of the exercise? What did you notice? What stood out? You might include emotions, bodily sensations, thoughts, perceptions or memories:
What was difficult in the exercise? What blocks or problems did you experience? How did you overcome them?
What did you find helpful about the exercise? What did you value? Why?
From your own experience, have you gained any insights into how clients might experience the intervention/practice? Think about your current caseload and bring to mind one of your clients and consider how your experience might have an effect on your attitude and/or your behaviour with this client:
Do your experiences and reflections have any implications for your practice as a CBT therapist? How might you introduce or undertake the exercise in the future? What will you change in your practice? Why?

In addition to the BE, Ramesh used a combination of macro and micro-skills to address these therapy-interfering behaviours

- *Administered the Alignment to CBT scale (Appendix 5) to address long term suitability for using CBT*
- *Introduced the concept of 'therapist schemas' (Leahy, 2001) to help Tom gain some distance from and curiosity about his habitual responses in therapy*

After a supervisee has completed an SP/SR exercise they should be encouraged to formally reflect on what they have learned and how they can carry this learning 'across the reflective bridge' (from therapist self to personal self or vice versa). The supervisor could provide a form with prompts similar to those in Table 16.1.

Keeping supervisees safe during SP/SR

SP/SR research has consistently found that a minority of participants find the experience aversive (Haarhoff et al., 2015). There are a number of 'safeguards' that we can put in place to minimise the risk of SP/SR feeling overwhelming:

- Working within their Zone of Proximal development (Vygotsky, 1978)
- Picking cognitions that generate moderate affect (e.g. staying in the 'Goldilocks zone'/window of tolerance)

- Safe Place imagery
- Generating a Safety Plan (e.g. take a break if necessary, schedule pleasant/immersive activities after the task, discuss with supervisor, consider personal therapy)

Therapist schemas

Separate to SP/SR, Leahy (2001) developed a therapist schema questionnaire (TS) which identified fifteen 'therapist schemas' based on his own experiences as a clinician and his observations as a trainer and supervisor of Cognitive Behavioural practitioners. These TS may account for problems that CBT supervisors often encounter, such as therapist anxiety about upsetting or offending their clients.

Haarhoff (2006) sought to generate evidence for therapist schemas and administered the Therapist Schema Questionnaire (TSQ) to four groups of CBT trainees in New Zealand (n = 64). The three most common schemas irrespective of whether the trainees were near the beginning or end of their training were 'demanding standards' (e.g. 'I must cure all of my patients'), 'excessive self-sacrifice' (e.g. the patient's needs are more important than my own') and 'special superior person' (e.g. 'I am entitled to be successful').

It can be useful to ask your supervisees to complete the TSQ during supervision or as a homework task so that you can both try to spot their highest scoring schemas within their clinical work or within supervision. This could be used as an SP/SR exercise, or it can be used in a less formal way (e.g. 'let's try and spot these schemas as and when they show up in future supervision sessions'). The following set of questions can help to 'open up' general discussions around how we as therapists can 'get in our own way' during treatment.

Reflective exercise

Recognising TS in your supervisees – questions for supervisors

Do you feel as if you have to 'fix' all of your clients?
Do you get upset, defensive, withdraw if a client becomes angry with you?
Do you need your clients to like you?

Broadening the schema concept

Therapist schemas as described by Leahy (2001) seem to locate the problem within the individual, almost as if one has a psychological 'Achilles heel'. Conversely, we might view therapist schemas as transient and context dependent,

Table 16.2 Therapist schema types

Schema Type	*Schema content*
Contextual schemas	e.g. 'we don't do those types of interventions here'/'we don't do that in supervision'
Training schemas	e.g. 'this is how CBT is done' 'it's habituation or the highway!'
Previous Professional role-related schemas	e.g. 'I should never interrupt a client'
Supervisor/supervisee schemas	e.g. 'supervision is exposing' 'supervision only covers Y'

rather than cognitive structures that are fixed, 'individual deficits'. For example, Roscoe and Taylor (2023) outline at least four other potential schema types (see Table 16.2). To pick one example of this, contextual factors (such as service demands) have been underexplored but may account for the development of some therapist schemas. A therapist's schema profile might change considerably when they move from an NHS setting to private practice. Their 'demanding standards' schema could be largely influenced by the demands of their employer rather a reflection on how they approach their work on the whole. Furthermore, some schemas might 'ease off' with greater clinical experience (e.g. 'Helplessness') therefore it would be important to understand which schemas are more pervasive across the career span.

When do therapist schemas become problematic?

Roscoe and Taylor (2023) have proposed that maladaptive therapist schemas refer to

> any recurring and inflexible cognitions that lead to either emotional difficulties for the therapist (e.g. anxiety, fear, anger, or shame) or to behaving in ways with clients that risk ruptures, boundary violations, or therapy and supervision being delivered in a sub-optimal fashion (e.g. frequent ruptures, inappropriate self-disclosures or avoiding, delaying or being excessively cautious with certain interventions.
>
> (p4–5)

Basma was working with a client who had a chaotic attendance pattern, attending one week then cancelling the next. This client also failed to complete homework tasks and would often interrupt her when she was speaking in session and go off on tangents. Basma felt frustrated and dominated by the client and therapy felt like it was going nowhere. This was backed up by the scores remaining high on the routine outcome measures. Despite this, Basma felt reluctant to raise her concerns with the client. When this case was discussed in supervision, Ramesh asked Basma to consider if these barriers were down to a skills gap (e.g. not knowing how to contain the client) or due to one or more TS. Basma completed the TSQ and reflected afterwards that she knew what she was supposed to do, but her TS led her into self-sacrificing and unassertive behaviour with this client.

Steps for introducing TS work within supervision

1. Introduce the concept of therapist schemas to normalise their existence and interference
2. Administer the Therapist Schema Questionnaire (TSQ) in supervision or as a homework task
3. Discuss responses by considering clinical scenarios or supervision situations where these schemas might be activated (consider linking to information gathered within the pre-supervision questionnaire; see Chapter 10)
4. Bring the supervisee's attention to the schemas if you notice it in their clinical work or within supervision
5. Help them to consider the consequences of 'fusing' with the schema
6. Consider introducing the concept of 'modes' or 'parts' as cognitive-emotional states that lead to therapy or supervision-interfering behaviours (this primes them for chair work)
7. Problem solve how the supervisee can learn to spot these schemas in real time (through the use of mindful awareness and/or self-practice of CBT methods)

Questions for meta-supervision

I'm new to the concept of SP/SR where do I begin try to incorporate it within supervision?

My supervisee has stated that they are unwilling to discuss personal material, what should I do next?

Chapter summary

- Self-Practice and Self-Reflection (SP/SR) deepen CBT learning by allowing therapists to experience interventions personally, bridging theory and practice.
- Supervisees select a personal or professional that is linked to real clinical challenges and reflect formally on insights and implications for their practice.
- Therapists own schemas can interfere with therapy and supervision therefore the TSQ (Therapist Schema Questionnaire) can be used to identify and address problematic schemas.

- Supervisors should be mindful of the emotional impact of supervisees working with their own material and put appropriate safeguards in place.

Recommended reading

Haarhoff, B. A. (2006). The importance of identifying and understanding therapist schema in cognitive therapy training and supervision. *New Zealand Journal of Psychology*, 35, 126–131.

Chapter 17

Identifying and responding to therapist drift

Introduction

If you were to open a classic CBT textbook and read some of the vignettes, it can seem remarkably quick and simple to help a client change their (often longstanding) beliefs. Demonstrations from tutors in lectures are often done in relation to 'straight forward' presentations of a specific disorder, adding to the idea that therapy, if done correctly will work like magic. This can lead those who are new to CBT into believing that if they ask the 'right questions' in the right way then their clients will have these wonderful 'eureka moments', leading to rapid and enduring symptom relief.

Of course, the reality is that therapy can often feel like two steps forward and one step back or even worse, that it is not moving at all. When CBT does not 'work' in the way we hope it will, this can lead some practitioners into blaming themselves, the client or the approach itself.

We often think of therapy-interfering behaviours that our clients engage in, such as avoiding homework tasks, arguing for why their beliefs are true and why we cannot help them (Leahy, 2008). This chapter is devoted to understanding therapist-initiated therapy-interfering behaviours.

When the problem is you

It is rarely as simple as it being the therapist or client who is 'at fault' for therapy drifting away from its core aims. However, one common therapist response to getting stuck with a client is to abandon the structure of CBT and just listen and nod as the client mindlessly tells you about different problems from session to session. When we collude (e.g. 'it's true their circumstances are too dire for them to change') or 'give up' (e.g. "I'll just let the client talk as they are not ready to change"), we are no longer providing CBT, and the client is certainly not receiving an evidence-based treatment (see Waller, 2009). An important point to make is that CBT is not a 'fix all' approach, and therefore not every client will benefit, regardless of how experienced and competent a therapist is. This does not mean that we 'down tools', it is important to either suggest that the client consider a different type of therapy or take the case to supervision to problem solve where things have become stuck.

DOI: 10.4324/9781003590620-20

Supervisor tip

We might also abandon or delay core aspects of CBT because we feel overwhelmed by the list of problems or how they relate to each other. Another reason is that therapists reject aspects of CBT as a person level, such as fearing that certain methods will make the client worse (Schulte & Eifert, 2002).

What is therapist drift?

Therapist drift is said to occur when therapists either knowingly or unknowingly avoid, delay or water-down interventions, compromising the effectiveness of the treatment (Waller, 2009). For example, weighing clients each session is a core component of CBT for Eating Disorders, yet surveys indicate that this is regularly avoided due to fears of the client's or one's own distress (D'Souza Walsh et al., 2019). My experiences of supervising therapists and reviewing the literature on this topic suggests that therapist drift arises for one of four reasons:

- The fear of making the client worse
- A fear of upsetting or offending the client
- The belief that CBT is insufficient for the client and needs to be augmented in some way
- The supervisee's beliefs about what constitutes CBT

The fear of making the client worse

Avoidance of exposure-based interventions is well documented within the literature (e.g. Meyer et al., 2014, 2020). Many trainees (and some qualified therapists) believe that interventions such as imaginal exposure or in vivo exposure will retraumatise clients or make their symptoms worse (Purnell et al., 2024). To elicit these concerns, we can ask the supervisee to complete a measure such as the Negative Beliefs about CBT Scale (Parker & Waller, 2017) or the Alignment to CBT scale (see Appendix 5). These can promote curiosity, potentially circumventing a defensive reaction from the supervisee. It is important to point out that negative beliefs don't always translate into avoidant behaviour. Some therapists will adhere to a treatment protocol but worry that they are making the client worse or that they have upset the client in some way. Nevertheless, persistent negative beliefs or poor alignment with CBT as a modality, coupled with observations of poor adherence (e.g. when reviewing video recordings) should prompt the supervisor to consider that drift is taking place. Therapist perfectionism or intolerance of uncertainty can also lead them to procrastinating because they are not absolutely sure how an intervention will go (Roscoe & Taylor, 2023).

> The idea of using 'reliving' with clients who have PTSD felt scary for Tom and having previously experienced social anxiety, he dreaded the idea of having to do 'bandwidth broadening' experiments as part of training such as deliberately doing something 'silly' in public to gauge how others respond.

Fear of upsetting or offending the client

Some therapists, especially trainees, are preoccupied with the fear of upsetting or angering their clients. Agenda setting, a core aspect of the structure of CBT is often seen as invalidating and restrictive and can be avoided or skirted over by some therapists. Interrupting clients is often unavoidable as we need to socialise them to therapy and help them get the most out of each session. Many therapists worry that in doing so, they are invalidating the client and as a result of this, they might let a client ramble on for a whole session without focusing them. Leahy (2001) identified a list of 'therapist schemas' which capture some of the core fears underpinning this behaviour. For example, therapists with a 'rejection-sensitive' schema will do all they can to avoid conflict with their clients (and their supervisor for that matter!).

The belief that CBT is insufficient for the client and needs to be augmented in some way

Some therapists believe that CBT only works for simple problems and that when a client presents with co-morbidity or complexity they need to shift to a different approach (e.g. counselling) or augment CBT with third wave approaches or elements of them (e.g. mindfulness strategies). On a case-by-case basis, both of these beliefs might be warranted, and it is important to consider the difference between applying meta-competencies and drifting (Roscoe & Campbell-Lee, 2025).

Attitudes towards aspects of CBT

The requirement for 'fidelity' to the model that exists within CBT might be at odds with other approaches that seemingly welcome theoretical integration and eclecticism (e.g. Beaumont & Hollins Martin, 2013). This 'fidelity demand' can jar with existing therapist beliefs about how therapy is best delivered, especially if individuals have worked in a more integrative way prior to training in CBT. Alternatively, many therapists place more value on their clinical experiences of what works and what does not (Roscoe, 2020b). Consequently, some therapists may 'resist' what they see as a 'purist' or 'manualised' approach to CBT, which they feel is lacking in something or too rigid. There are two problematic ends of the spectrum here, the first end being those who hold very negative beliefs about CBT (e.g. CBT only focuses on 'the here and now' or CBT does not address 'the root of the problem' (Parker & Waller, 2017) whilst the opposite end is where individuals hold very rigid beliefs about what CBT is designed to treat and what interventions can be used at any given time.

Some of these beliefs are based on half-truths (e.g. CBT predominantly focuses on the here and now but will focus on the past when necessary) and some are based on misconceptions (e.g. it is simply wrong that the root of a problem is always based in the distant past, as with the case of Panic Disorder). Furthermore, CBT uses a range of methods that address the impact of early life events such as reliving and rescripting. Critics often use this as a straw man argument to sleight CBT, however CBT therapists can also contribute to claims of its superficiality by denying clients access to treatment because they do not fit neatly into a diagnostic category. Below are some examples of how Sonia and Ramesh developed their beliefs about CBT.

> Sonia has been supervised by several individuals during her career as a clinical psychologist. Some of her previous supervisors held very 'anti-CBT' views, whereas others had helped her to see how it could be used flexibly whilst retaining fidelity to the cognitive model. This has helped Sonia to learn which style and methods seem to work for her and those she supervises. Sonia is trained in Schema Therapy and Dialectical Behaviour Therapy in addition to CBT, but is very careful about how she uses these in her own clinical practice, being vigilant for signs of her supervisees straying too far from the CBT model.
>
> Ramesh has only ever worked within a Primary Care context and is highly influenced by disorder-specific models. During his CBT training, the supervisors that he encountered were very strict on determining which clients were suited to CBT and which were not. As a new supervisor, Ramesh is quick to advise his supervisees about whether certain clients are suitable for CBT, based on them fitting the description of an anxiety disorder or depression and how that compares with one of these models.

The supervisee's beliefs about what constitutes CBT

A fair proportion of individuals that enter CBT training have had experience of delivering it in some shape or form. This means that they already have a 'CBT schema' which tells them what constitutes a CBT formulation or intervention. Undoubtedly, this means that supervisees will hold one or more misconceptions that need to be addressed (Murray et al., 2022) and some bad habits that they have developed. This can involve routinely adding techniques in that belong to other approaches (without a clear rationale) and missing out important techniques. These beliefs and behaviours might have been reinforced in previous supervisory relationships. Occasionally, poor teaching practices or more often, a lack of exposure to working with certain type of cases during training (e.g. not treating PTSD until qualified) can mean that supervisees have faulty beliefs about how to deliver CBT or aspects of it.

> It became apparent to her supervisor, Sonia, that Trudie was not doing reliving when treating clients with PTSD. When reviewing the case conceptualisation in supervision, Trudie was always vague about what aspects of the Ehlers and

Clark model she was referring to and seemed to avoid showing a written formulation when presenting PTSD cases. Trudie seemed to focus on behavioural activation and mindfulness meditation. When discussing the rationale for selecting these interventions, it seemed that the function was to help her client avoid painful memories rather than face them and update them. When Sonia raised this with Trudie she became defensive and stated that this is what she had been taught to do during her training.

Reflective exercise

Understanding your own journey into CBT

How do you use CBT within your own work as a therapist? What factors have influenced this? (e.g. style and content of CBT training you received, supervisors past and present, client group)

If you integrate CBT with other approaches, what is your rationale for this?

If you use CBT as a standalone approach, what is your rationale for this?

Noticing drift in supervision

We might notice signs of therapist drift as a result of the following within supervision:

- Through observing video recordings/listening to audio recordings of our supervisee's therapy sessions
- From reviewing formulations or treatment plans that are shared within supervision
- By observing what the supervisee does/avoids doing during re-enactments or other types of role-play
- Through noticing recurrent objections to core aspects of CBT (e.g. formulation or interventions)

Responding to drift

The CBT supervisor has several options available to them once they notice drift in their supervisee's practice. The first is to do nothing other than note it and see if there are spontaneous changes over the next few weeks and months. Further reading, demonstrations from the supervisor, teaching sessions or clinical contact might result in a correction in supervisee behaviour. The second option is to gently explore beliefs that might be contributing towards drift, using the measures described earlier and which encourage the supervisee to reflect on the consequences of avoiding or delaying key aspects of treatment. The supervisor could offer to model the delivery of certain interventions to increase supervisee confidence and follow this up with role-play or deliberate practice (see Chapter 15). The other option, which is usually a last resort, is taking steps to intervene in the interests of client safety (e.g. if the supervisee is displaying unethical behaviour). This might involve liaising with the supervisee's line manager and on occasion, informing accrediting bodies such as the BABCP about fitness to practice concerns.

Questions for meta-supervision

I suspect that my supervisee is drifting on a regular basis. How do I raise this with them without is causing a rupture?

There are certain CBT techniques that I avoid too. I feel like a hypocrite telling my supervisees that they need to use them. What should I do in these circumstances?

Chapter summary

- Therapist drift is normal and likely to be common, especially when individuals are new to using CBT. Clinical Complexity or therapist beliefs might trigger drift, and supervisors should be vigilant for signs of drift when reviewing the work of their supervisees.
- We should not assume that drift is only a problem that occurs amongst trainees, meaning that reviewing recordings of qualified therapists remains an important part of supervision.
- It is important to understand the function of therapist drift; is the supervisee using meta-competencies to adapt treatment to the needs of the client or are they deliberately avoiding key aspects of formulation or treatment?

Recommended reading

Speers, A. J., Bhullar, N., Cosh, S., & Wootton, B. M. (2022). Correlates of therapist drift in psychological practice: A systematic review of therapist characteristics. *Clinical Psychology Review*, 93, 102132. https://doi.org/10.1016/j.cpr.2022.102132

Chapter 18

Identifying and managing supervision-interfering behaviours

Introduction

Previous chapters have shown how supervisors must often encourage their supervisees to move out of their comfort zones through showing recordings of their work or by engaging in an exercise such as deliberate practice (Boswell & Constantino, 2021). Many supervisees embrace these challenges by accepting the anxiety and self-criticism that often go hand in hand with these exercises. Despite this, there will be times where the CBT supervisor is faced with persistent avoidance of certain tasks, or their suggestions are met with covert or overt resistance. It might be tempting to 'back off' when met with one or more challenges as a way of preserving the supervisory relationship (Pugh & Margetts, 2020). The fear of increasing the supervisee's anxiety or of causing a rupture can mean that supervisors allow these supervisees to 'rule the roost' (e.g. dominating supervision sessions with case discussion). This comes at a great cost, as in doing so, it means that supervision will (in all likelihood) fail to achieve its normative, formative or restorative functions (Proctor, 1994).

This chapter is concerned with how we might identify and manage persistent avoidance, where more subtle attempts to elicit supervision supporting behaviours (SSBs) have failed. It also addresses the problems that arise from an unwavering resistance to elements of CBT that may culminate in defensive behaviour, all of which ultimately inhibit therapist skill development.

Reflection exercise

Reducing the chances of SIBS

Bring to mind a supervisee who has persistently avoided certain tasks within supervision.

Does this supervisee feel safe enough to disclose information to you?

DOI: 10.4324/9781003590620-21

Could there be some misconceptions or fears at the root of avoidant or resistant behaviour?
Have you made sufficient efforts to normalise supervision-interfering and therapy-interfering behaviours and to create space to separate this from the 'person' of the supervisee?

Understanding SIBS

In contrast to the SSBs that have been addressed elsewhere in the book, avoidance, defensiveness and resistance can be considered to be supervision-interfering behaviours (SIBS). For example, the avoidant supervisee continues to provide reasons why recordings of their work cannot be shown (e.g. client refusal, tech issues), whilst the defensive supervisee may try to engage the supervisor in debate or offer reasons as to why their suggestions will not work with their clients.

Supervisee avoidance

For many, avoidance is an understandable yet transient phase at the start of training or at the start of a new supervisory relationship. Once the supervisee gets more comfortable with the supervisor, they are likely to bring a video clip and find out that the feedback is nowhere near as bad as their mind was telling them it would be. However, the power differential or the lasting effect of previous supervisory relationships can mean that some supervisees do not move beyond this phase. They may or may not verbalise their thoughts and emotions to the supervisor, but the end product is the same – the supervisor remains mostly 'in the dark' about their actual clinical work.

Defensiveness

Other supervisees may adopt a more confrontational stance to the situation through acts of overt or covert resistance (e.g. refusing to use certain methods with their clients or within supervision) or displays of defensiveness in the face of actual or perceived criticism. Defensiveness is often characterised by confrontation whereby the supervisee might refuse to accept the supervisor's feedback or recommendations but may also result in them questioning the supervisor's experience, knowledge or credentials. Covert resistance can be more difficult to spot but may be characterised by the supervisee agreeing with the supervisor within supervision but then disregarding their advice and doing what they want with their clients. Table 18.1 provides a non-exhaustive list of examples of how a supervisor might spot avoidant or defensive SIBS during their interactions with supervisees.

Table 18.1 Supervision-interfering behaviours

Types of avoidance	*Types of defensiveness*
Supervisees may avoid tasks (e.g. videos of sessions) because of the feared outcome (e.g. failure/humiliation)	Rivalry – competing with the supervisor Debating
Emotional/experiential avoidance (avoiding tasks because they generate 'negative' emotions or aversive physical sensations)	Hostile Criticism of the Supervisor Refusing to accept feedback
Withdrawing (there but not there)	
Non-disclosure	

Understanding the drivers of supervisee avoidance, resistance or defensiveness

Both avoidance and defensiveness can signal either intentional or unintentional 'resistance' towards CBT as a therapy or certain requirements of supervision. I propose that we tend to encounter two types of resistance.

Intentional resistance –when a supervisee openly rejects aspects of CBT or supervision on ethical, schematic or epistemic grounds (e.g. Lee et al., 2013).

Unintentional resistance –when a supervisee reverts to using 'tried and tested' methods of conceptualising or treating clinical problems in the face of uncertainty or anxiety (e.g. Roscoe et al., 2022b).

Sonia had noticed across several supervision sessions that Sonny appeared to hold a range of negative beliefs about CBT. He would often question the ethical nature of interventions such as reliving or exposure and response prevention (ERP) and stated that he preferred to take a less directive and more supportive approach to his clinical work.

Ramesh noticed that Tom seemed to struggle with setting agendas with his clients. Tom worried that he would appear rude and invalidating if he stopped clients from talking and would oscillate between passivity and a didactic style where he would tell his clients what they need to do.

These examples provide a contrast between Sonny's overt rejection of aspects of CBT and Tom's anxiety, which leads him to engage in behaviours that are counterproductive to the aims of CBT. Clearly, they will require different interventions from Ramesh and Sonia. For Ramesh, he can help Tom to learn how to pause clients in a compassionate way or develop behavioural experiments to test Tom's predictions that his clients will think him rude and invalidating (see Chapter 16).

For Sonia, it would be worthwhile exploring the 'intrapersonal conflict' that Sonny is experiencing (Wilcockson, 2020). This might involve educating him on some of his misconceptions about the aims and outcomes of CBT methods such as reliving or ERP (Murray et al., 2022).

Options for managing SIBS

In addition to the bespoke supervisory interventions described above, there are a range of 'generic' options available to supervisors for handling SIBS. Each have their respective advantages and disadvantages, and we can employ the familiar skill of problem–solving, whereby we list every option that is available, regardless of how useful it is, before moving on to weigh up the pros and cons of each. Some options that are available to supervisors are listed below.

- Ignore the behaviour and hope it goes away (not recommended, but in the spirit of keeping an open mind at this stage!)
- Address the behaviour directly in the moment (e.g. use an active method to identify, isolate, analysis and change the SIBS)
- Refer to relevant details in the pre-supervision questionnaire/contract (see Chapter 10)
- Use Alliance or 'alignment' measures to gauge the presence/strength of potential difficulties (see Chapter 12; Appendix 5)
- Plan a behavioural experiment
- Formulate the problem relating to the supervisee (see Chapter 19)

Supervisor tip

If you decide to ignore the behaviour, it is worth deciding in advance how many supervision sessions you will allow the SIB to continue before switching tactics.

The order in which these tactics are listed could work well as a process of gradual escalation. For example, having let a behaviour go in one session, if the supervisor notices that it continues across several sessions, they could name the SIB there and then or review the Pre-Supervision Questionnaire answers to understand their attitudes towards different methods. A behavioural experiment could form part of the supervision session or be developed as a homework task before feeling the need to explicitly formulate the behaviour.

Table 18.2 provides a seven-step procedure for responding to persistent SIBS, with prompts for supervisors to consider at each step. Steps 1 and 2 could guide the

Table 18.2 Seven-step procedure for responding to persistent SIBS

Step 1: Identify the behaviour	What am I observing in the session?
Step 2: Notice your reactions	What thoughts do I experience about the supervisee and about myself? How do I feel? What do I have the urge to do in response to their behaviour?
Step 3: Formulate either on your own, with your meta-supervisor or with the supervisee (if there is not too much 'heat')	Explore the functions and history of reinforcement (e.g. how have previous supervisors responded to this behaviour?) Use the information from the Pre-supervision questionnaire to hypothesise causal factors (if this information has been captured) N.B. It might be necessary to work on understanding your own supervision-interfering behaviours before moving on to step 4
Step 4: Address the specific behaviour assertively and promptly	Put the SIB on the agenda to discuss Avoid blaming language (e.g. use 'I feel' rather than 'you make me feel')
Step 5: Use empathic confrontation	Validate their fears/discomfort, formulate with them your understanding of why it might be difficult to do/stop doing specific things Empathise with challenges, model your own vulnerability, explain why the behaviour needs to change
Step 6: Agree a plan for changing the behaviour	This might involve recapping the rationale for active methods; supervisor modelling; identifying specific therapist schemas to modify/look out for in future sessions (Leahy, 2001), setting up behavioural experiments for the supervisee, chair work to increase capacity for de-centring from 'parts' of the client that are involved in the behaviour (see Chapter 20)
Step 7: Review the outcome	Has this changed the aggressive, defensive or avoidant behaviour? If not, return to step 3 or consider using another method to address the SIBS

supervisor in starting to fill out the model that is described within Chapter 19 (as either a self-supervision exercise, within meta-supervision or with the supervisee).

Retaining the balance between safety and challenge within the relationship

As with therapeutic relationships, addressing interpersonal processes in supervision such as supervisee avoidance or resistance carries the potential of causing or (initially) worsening a rupture (Samstag et al., 2003). Supervisors must balance the risk of broaching the SIB with the risk of letting it continue. Rather than viewing ruptures as something to be avoided at all costs, we can view them with curiosity, and formulating them as described in the next chapter can help both parties to deepen their understanding of CBT, through applying it to themselves.

Questions for meta-supervision

It feels awkward to challenge my supervisee's avoidance. How can I do this without making it seem a 'big deal'?

Chapter summary

- The evaluative nature of supervision is inherently threatening, leading to understandable feelings of anxiety, fear, shame and embarrassment.
- These emotions and beliefs about oneself and the supervisor are more heightened in some supervisees than others (e.g. those prone to perfectionism or experiential avoidance).
- For many supervisees, avoidance is a transient phase at the start of training or at the start of a new supervisory relationship.
- The PSQ (see Chapter 10) can help the supervisor to anticipate SIBS that may arise within the relationship.
- Being open to and about feedback, being willing to change and reducing the power differential where possible helps to strengthen the supervisory relationship.

Recommended reading

Nelson, M. L., Barnes, K. L., Evans, A. L., & Triggiano, P. J. (2008). Working with conflict in clinical supervision: Wise supervisors' perspectives. *Journal of Counseling Psychology*, 55(2), 172.

Chapter 19

Formulating and managing avoidant, resistant or defensive supervisee behaviour

Introduction

Previous chapters have discussed how we might identify and respond to supervision-interfering behaviours (SIBS). For example, frequent use of alliance measures such as the Leeds Alliance in Supervision Scale (LASS; Wainwright, 2010) and working through the seven-step procedure (see Chapter 18) can generate discussions about and stop these SIBS from becoming ingrained within the supervisory relationship. The assumption taken in this chapter is that previous steps have failed to curb the SIB and that the supervisor has recognised specific consequences of them continuing to have an influence in future sessions.

The benefits of formulation

Formulating differences between supervisor and supervisee offers a gentler (and CBT congruent) way of addressing problems head on without accusation or shaming the other person. In contrast to simply having a conversation, formulation can take the 'heat' out of any exchange, with the primary focus being on the piece of paper or electronic document (if the session is online) that is being shared. It can also evoke curiosity with both parties, rather than allocating blame. More importantly perhaps, it provides the supervisor with the opportunity to model how to manage conflicts and how to structure difficult conversations. Nelson et al. (2008) summarise this nicely by stating that 'if a supervisor handles the situation well, then the supervisee is provided with an opportunity to learn critical lessons about how to manage conflict situations with clients in a healing and educational, rather than harmful, way' (p172).

Supervisory schemas

Before we start to formulate what is going on during any given supervision session, it is important for us to understand how supervisors and supervisees construct their mental template of what supervision and is and how it should be conducted. These 'schemas' are informed by the 3 C's as discussed in Chapter 8 (culture, context

DOI: 10.4324/9781003590620-22

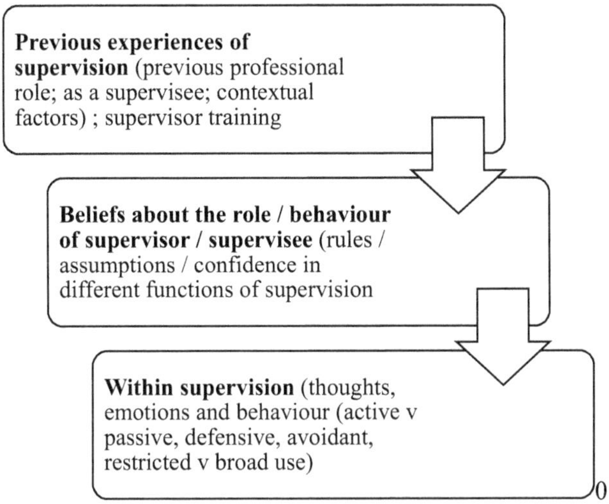

Figure 19.1 Supervisory schema development.

and cognitions) and become a lens through which we experience the supervisor or supervisees behaviour in the 'here and now'. Figure 19.1 offers a visual representation of the ways in which our past experiences of supervision shape our beliefs about supervision and prime us to think, feel and behave in certain ways in supervision sessions.

Supervisor tip

Supervisors and supervisees will vary in terms of their awareness of factors that are influencing their supervisory schemas. In fact, a supervisor might wish to try and map out their own formulation before doing this with a supervisee.

The contents of Figure 19.1 are very much in keeping with the generic longitudinal cognitive model (Beck et al., 1979). Formulating SIBS from this perspective provides a common language that makes sense to CBT therapists. For example, this model was piloted with 32 CBT supervisors, and there was a high level of face validity amongst their responses to a follow-up survey (Roscoe, 2021c). Formulation allows the CBT supervisor to incorporate familiar terminology (e.g. negative automatic thoughts, rules and assumptions, safety behaviours), and it provides a trusted framework for making sense of stuck points within supervision.

Chapter 18 summarises the types of SIBS that CBT supervisors are likely to come across, yet many of us struggle with conflict and defer to people pleasing and avoidance as a means of avoiding confrontation (Leahy, 2001). As difficult as it might feel, there are compelling reasons to address rather than avoid SIBS. Firstly, persistent avoidance prevents the supervisor from making a well-informed judgment about the supervisee's skillset.

> Sonia had noticed that Trudie did not volunteer to bring recordings of her clinical work to supervision and seemed to provide a range of excuses for why this was not possible when pressed on the issue. Sonia explained that without viewing some aspects of her work, it was difficult to fulfil her normative and formative duties as her supervisor.

Secondly, by showing a willingness to broach difficult conversations, the supervisor is modelling the ways their supervisee might address similar processes with their clients (Nelson et al., 2008).

Sonia: I'm just reflecting on the last few times that we have discussed bringing videos to supervision and you know, it feels anxiety provoking for me to raise this, as I don't want to make this a big issue, however, it is crucial for me to be a responsible supervisor and part of that is viewing your work.

Trudie: I know, I get it, I just think I've got out of the habit of recording or asking clients for consent to record, it feels like a hassle that I could do without.

Sonia: I understand how pressured your service is and as you say, recording can fall down the list of priorities but what would be the benefits for you in starting to record again?

Why and how to formulate SIBS

One of the first challenges for CBT supervisors is knowing where to start, and conversations like the one between Sonia and Trudie are one way of addressing 'the elephant in the room'. Contemporary models of CBT supervision have been helpful in explaining the functions of supervision and associated tasks (e.g. Armstrong & Freeston, 2006; Milne & Dunkerley, 2010) yet offered very little to help make sense of ruptures, transference and supervisory drift. Similarly, standard CBT formulations capture the individual perspective rather than recognising the reciprocal nature of problems such as collusion (Milne et al., 2009).

Interpersonal process model of CBT Supervision

The reciprocal model (Roscoe, 2021c) that is used within this chapter is influenced by two studies which looked at supervisor and supervisee expectations and behaviours (Roscoe, 2021c; Roscoe et al., 2022a), the existing supervision literature (e.g. Milne et al., 2009; Moorey & Lavender, 2019) and from listening to supervisor and supervisee feedback during supervisor training events. The model is, in essence, an 'action research' project – that is, it is continually evolving based on supervisor and supervisee feedback on using it (Koshy et al., 2011). This had led to various adaptations since its inception, such as adding or removing boxes to the diagram as appropriate. Examples of how the model can be used flexibly are mentioned, but detailed illustrations or descriptions are beyond the scope of this chapter.

Model overview

The model follows a traditional 'Beckian' longitudinal conceptualisation by proposing that the supervision dyad are influenced by a range of pre-disposing and cultural/contextual factors, which silently guide the behaviour and expectations of each party. This includes past experiences of supervision, the influence of previous professional roles (e.g. social work) content of CBT training (e.g. emphasis on cognitive or behavioural models) and 'personal self' factors (e.g. one's tolerance for uncertainty). The model also considers the influences of broader, systemic and cultural factors (e.g. accrediting body guidelines; workplace attitudes; time constraints).

Using the model with your supervisees

It is important to keep this information to what is immediately relevant to the SIB, rather than listing every variable. For example, for some supervisees their 'personal self' therapist schemas (e.g. emotional inhibition) might be highly relevant, whilst for others, the contributing factor will be related to their previous professional role (e.g. their style of supervision when they were a mental health nurse). The formulation can also be expanded to include more information, such as therapist schemas or to separate personal, previous professional or co-existing 'therapist self' factors. Some supervisees might also appreciate salient aspects of their identity being included to consider the impact of neurodiversity/past or current mental health difficulties/experiences of racism/homophobia on how they feel and act in supervision.

It is hypothesised that the more divergence there is between the supervisor and supervisee's backgrounds, the more risk there is of a mismatch between supervisor and supervisee expectations of supervision. Of course, different backgrounds can be complementary (e.g. learning from each other); however, when these expectations are not verbalised and take the form of silent assumptions about the other's role (e.g. what they should or should not do), a rupture may ensue. Figure 19.2 illustrates how this model has been used to formulate difficulties that Ramesh experienced in relation to Tom and him adjusting to the differences between low and high-intensity supervision.

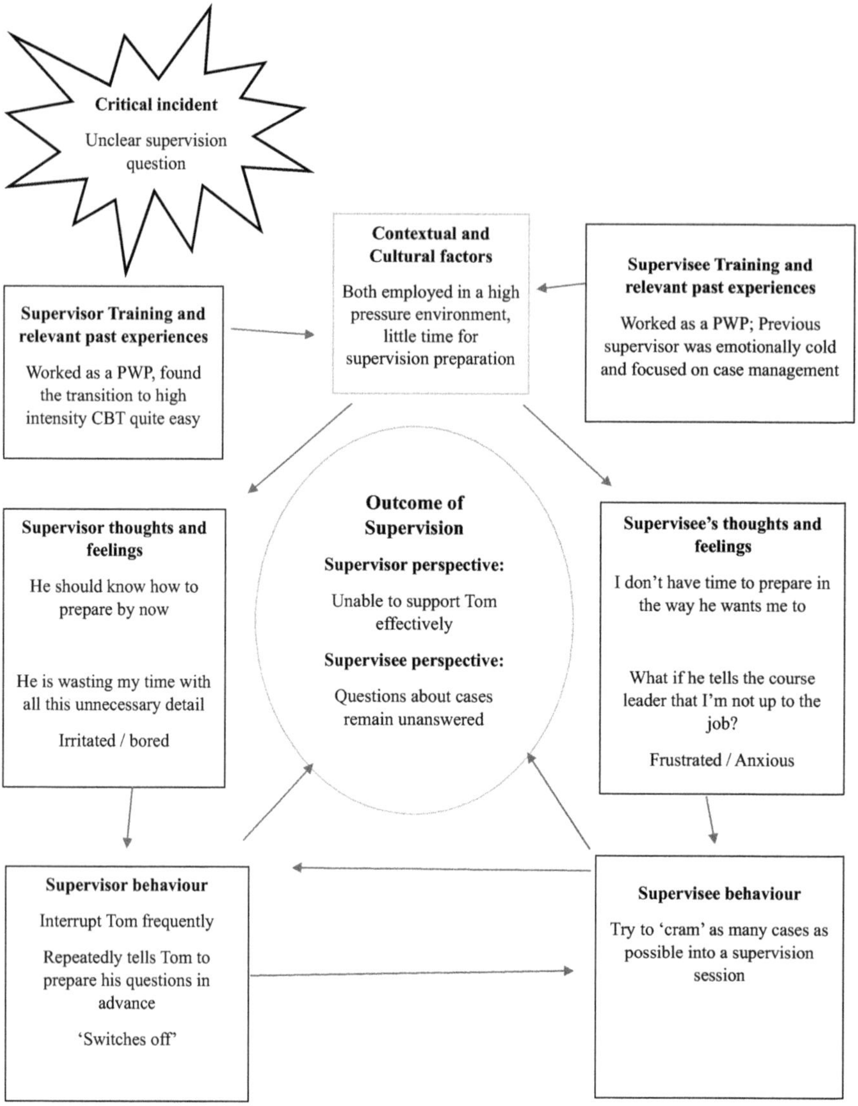

Figure 19.2 Interpersonal process model of CBT supervision.

Source: Roscoe, 2021c

Bringing the model to life

As the model illustrates, Tom and Ramesh were both experiencing irritation towards each other and frustration with the outcome of each supervision session. From Ramesh's point of view, Tom was not preparing adequately for supervision and felt that a lot of time was wasted in the session with superfluous details about the client. In contrast, Tom felt that Ramesh did not appreciate the time constraints that he was operating within and worried that Ramesh would judge him as unsuitable to work as a CBT therapist. Rather than expressing their thoughts and feelings about how they were experiencing supervision, both parties continued to behave in ways that appeared to 'pull' unhelpful responses from one another. For example, the more cases Tom tried to discuss in the supervision session, the more Ramesh felt the need to interrupt him to elicit a clear supervision question, yet the more Ramesh did this, the more invalidated Tom felt. Due to the 'heat' this generated for Ramesh, he decided to test out constructing the formulation in his own meta-supervision.

Reflective exercise

Is there a supervisee that you have had a rupture or difference of opinion with?
Could you try to map out this problem using the formulation in this chapter?

Adapting the model

The version in Figure 19.2 has been completed based on the information relating to both parties; however, it can be condensed to capture 'one half' of the dyad (e.g. to formulate just the supervisee or supervisor perspective). This can be helpful when the supervisor is concerned that an initial reciprocal formulation will not be well received and lead to further difficulties within the supervisory relationship. Alternatively, initially focusing on one member of the dyad can allow for a more detailed exploration of factors that are influencing their behaviour. Figure 19.3 shows the shortened version that was developed within meta-supervision.

In capturing this information, Ramesh was able to 'helicopter up' from his immediate negative automatic thoughts about Tom and to consider how he could change his own role in the maintenance of SIBs. When Ramesh explored their patterns of relating in the next supervision session, Tom was receptive to Ramesh formulating their joint experience of supervision, and this allowed them to understand each other's perspective and agree a way forward.

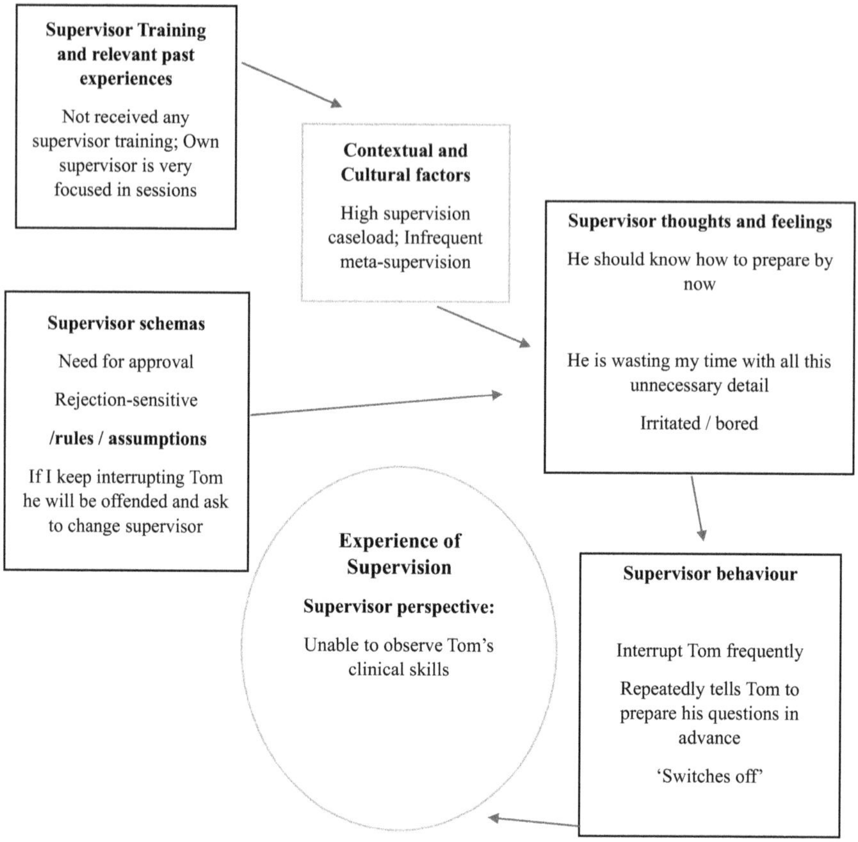

Figure 19.3 Supervisor-only version of the model.

Questions for meta-supervision

Is it better to formulate this problem with my supervisee or during meta-supervision?

What should I do if my supervisee gets angry or defensive after showing them the formulation?

Chapter summary

- This chapter addresses how supervisors can manage supervision-interfering behaviours (SIBs) when previous strategies have failed.

- It advocates for using formulation as a structured, CBT-congruent approach to reducing conflict and fostering curiosity rather than blame.
- Formulation provides a shared language and trusted CBT framework (e.g. automatic thoughts, rules, safety behaviours) and can help the dyad to decentre from their automatic reactions by providing a focal point.
- The formulation can be used flexibly (e.g. by mapping out a full dyad formulation or as a condensed version capturing supervisor or supervisee information only).

Recommended reading

Milne, D. L., Leck, C., & Choudhri, N. Z. (2009). Collusion in clinical supervision: Literature review and case study in self reflection. *The Cognitive Behaviour Therapist*, 2.

Chapter 20

Using chair work to embody different perspectives

Introduction

Chair work refers to a collection of techniques that involve the use of different chairs to encourage emotional expression or perspective taking within a therapy or supervision session (Pugh, 2019). The number of chairs used and their proximity to each other or to the client/supervisee will be determined not only by practicalities such as availability and space (e.g. room size) but also by the intended function of the exercise. This chapter looks at how chair work can help supervisors and supervisees to better understand certain aspects of themselves or their clients. This whistlestop tour of chair work will only 'skim the surface' of in terms of how these powerful methods can be used. Indeed, chair work is used across many therapies (see Ottingerová et al., 2026 for a more extensive overview); therefore, the concepts that are discussed here only reflect one 'pocket' of knowledge and are influenced by the recent work of Pugh and Bell (e.g. Pugh & Bell, 2020; Pugh et al., 2021), which has given it something of a renaissance amongst CBT therapists.

Reflective exercise

What are your own experiences of chair work as a therapist, supervisee or supervisor?

What are your beliefs about the value of chair work?

What is it, and why would we want to use chair work in supervision?

We often talk about helping clients to 'decentre' or 'helicopter up' from their automatic reactions, and as therapists and supervisors, we are no different in that we sometimes get 'hooked' by certain thoughts or emotions. If we struggle to decentre,

DOI: 10.4324/9781003590620-23

this can lead to us perpetuating unhelpful patterns of behaviour within therapy or supervision.

> Sonny initially struggled to decentre from his resistance towards aspects of CBT, including showing videos within supervision. This led to multiple 'standoffs' with his supervisor Sonia where she would continue to press for seeing evidence of his clinical work and he would 'push back' harder as to why he didn't agree with it.
>
> Sonia experienced Trudie as being quite 'cold' and 'matter of fact' during their interactions within supervision. Trudie seemed unaware at first of how her clients might experience her interpersonal style.

Shifting perspectives

There appears to be something about the physical act of standing up and changing seat or having the permission to fully adopt a specific perspective that seems to create more distance than one might achieve through a standard conversation. In short, chair work creates separation from a specific viewpoint (e.g. a belief or rule for living), and in doing so, it provides the opportunity to mindfully observe or magnify certain beliefs, emotions or behaviours. Bell et al. (2020) found that clients engaging in Compassion Focused Therapy reported the following benefits to engaging in chair work:

- Embodiment (e.g. taking on the role of another or a different 'part' of oneself)
- Externalising (being able to separate from a perspective during chair work)
- Movement (this facilitated the process of embodiment and externalisation)
- Accessing heightened emotions
- Seeing self as multiple parts
- Transformation and integration (e.g. resolving interpersonal or intrapersonal conflicts)

Whilst occupying different chairs to adopt different perspectives is not entirely new to CBT (see Beck, 1995) chair work has not been a key component of CBT training in the UK (BABCP, 2025), perhaps due to the intense focus on skilling therapists in the use of disorder-specific protocols. Whilst chair work does not feature in any of these, it is best to view chair work as a meta-competence (Roth & Pilling, 2007) and therefore a transdiagnostic tool which provides therapists with an experiential way of doing many of the standard interventions that are familiar to CBT therapists (see Table 20.1).

Where do I start with chair work?

If you have never used chair work in therapy, then it might feel quite intimidating to bring it into your supervision sessions. Whilst some basic training is advisable, the overarching principles of what needs to be present within a chair work exercise are outlined below, should you wish to try this active method.

Table 20.1 Standard CBT interventions with chair work alternatives

Standard CBT intervention	*Chair work alternative*
Written cost-benefit analysis	Moving back and forth between chairs, arguing the pros and cons of each option
Thought record	Speaking from the 'evidence for' and 'evidence against' in different chairs
Modifying positive beliefs about worry	Interviewing worry to find out what it 'does for the client' and then exploring how it works against the client

Pugh and Bell (2020) describe a combination of *principles* and *processes* that underpin effective chair work.

Principles

1 Self-Multiplicity – the idea that the 'self' is comprised of several 'I' positions that hold different beliefs, memories, emotions, bodily sensations and action tendencies
2 Information exchange – a dialogue is enacted between the different selves or between an aspect of self and therapist or supervisor
3 Transformation – there is some form of resolution following the information exchange

Processes

1 Separation – the therapist or supervisor actively facilitates the isolation of one of more 'selves' or 'parts' of the client or supervisee
2 Animation – this involves bringing the isolated part 'to life' by changing one's posture, tone of voice or belief/perspective that is being conveyed
3 Dialogue – a conversation is developed between either the therapist/supervisor and client/supervisee or between the client/supervisee and another part of themselves

Utility within supervision

Addressing problematic supervisee-client interactions

Chair work can be very helpful when supervisees are highly fused with a particular viewpoint. For example, that their client does not wish to change, and they are 'at fault' for the lack of progress within therapy.

> Trudie had brought the 'problem' of a client persistently failing to complete homework tasks to supervision. Sonia asked Trudie to move from the chair she

was sitting in to another one directly opposite and, in doing so, embody her client's perspective. Sonia then interviewed Trudie from the perspective of her client.

Sonia: Vikram, how do you feel when Trudie asks you about why you didn't complete your homework tasks?
Trudie (as Vikram): I feel like a schoolboy being told off by the teacher, I guess.
Sonia: And do you feel as if Sonia gives you the opportunity to provide this feedback?
Trudie (as Vikram): I don't think she has really explored the reasons why I don't do it, she just tells me how important homework is in CBT.

This role-play continued for a while longer, and afterwards Sonia and Trudie reflected on what learning had taken place as a result of this. Trudie stated that 'stepping into Vikram's shoes' gave her a chance to observe how others might experience her as a therapist. Trudie also reflected on her 'personal self', in that friends and family have said she sometimes seems 'curt' and 'unapproachable'.

As this chair work vignette demonstrates, supervisees can often emerge from these exercises with not only greater self-awareness but also greater empathy for their clients.

Addressing problematic supervisee-supervisor interactions

Similarly, moving chair and then speaking from an unvoiced 'part' of the self (e.g. the part of the supervisee that wants to avoid showing videos) can give permission for this part to exist and can also help the supervisor and supervisee to understand what will help to make this part feel safer. As supervisors, we should remain mindful that chair work could feel quite exposing and intimidating to some supervisees; therefore, it is worthwhile considering how you might 'warm them up' to the idea.

Normalise self-multiplicity

As supervisors we can normalise the concept of being 'in two minds' about something, such as 'part of you wants to show a video in supervision' (e.g. the 'wise part') and 'part of you does not' (the 'scared part').

Sonia: Sonny if we could speak to that part of you that really doesn't want to show recordings to me, what would it say?
Sonny: I guess it would say
Sonia: Let me stop you there Sonny, I'd like you to speak from that part so rather than 'I guess', be that part and tell me how you feel about this recording.

As the vignette between Sonia and Sonny highlights, chair work does not necessarily involve moving chairs at this point, but the supervisor should track how responsive and open the supervisee is to this, rather than feeling like they have to follow arbitrary steps. We can gradually encourage a supervisee to become more immersed in the embodiment of different 'parts' as time goes on.

Reinforce self-multiplicity and naming of parts across different supervision sessions

Having introduced self-multiplicity to supervision, Sonny will be less surprised if Sonia 'names' one of his avoidant or more helpful 'parts' in subsequent supervision sessions. For example, when Sonia asks Sonny to draw out a model in supervision, he looks visibly concerned. It can be helpful for the supervision dyad to agree a personally salient name for each part.

Sonia: Has anxious Sonny just popped up when I said that?"

Sonny: Yeah, I feel like I'm about to get found out for the imposter that I am [laughs]

Sonia: Don't worry, I'm not trying to catch you out. Does anxious Sonny work as a way of us identifying that part of you would you go with a different name?

Once Sonny is sufficiently 'socialised' to the concepts of chair work, Sonia can then invite him to move into a different chair to embody his anxious or avoidant part. If chair numbers or room size is an issue, then supervisees can move their chair to the left or right or closer or further away from the supervisor. Supervisors are directed to the journal paper by Pugh and Bell (2020), which provides guidance on how to adapt chair work for online working.

Supervisor tip

There are many potential advantages to using chair work with supervision, especially when we view therapist skill development through the lens of active methods. Most importantly, it shifts the supervisory exchange from talking about the supervision question to doing something in response to it. Chair work in that sense is ideal for facilitating the process of experiential learning (Kolb, 1984).

Linking chair work to other concepts of self-multiplicity

Visual aids can augment chair work, either as a primer (done beforehand) or to build on certain concepts afterwards. For example, the supervisor could use a sheet of paper, a whiteboard or, if sharing their screen online, an electronic document

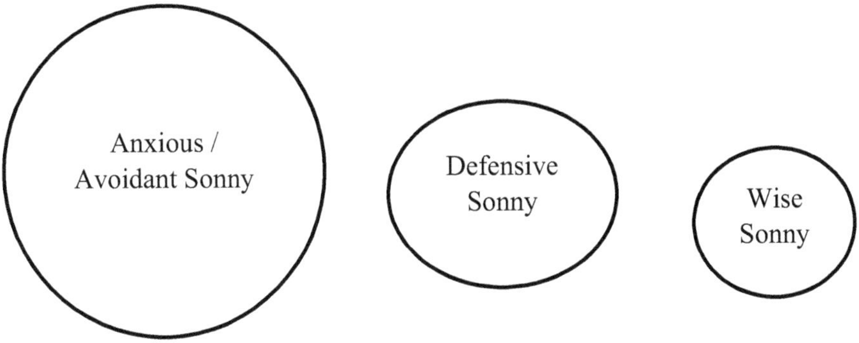

Figure 20.1 'Parts' map.

to help consider the 'size' or dominance of different parts of the supervisee. They could also indicate that a chair that is further away is a part that is less familiar to them or needs to be accessed more frequently.

Sonia used a series of circles to represent different 'parts' of Sonny that she had observed across numerous supervision sessions (see Figure 20.1). Sonia asked Sonny to describe which one was the most dominant in that session, and they discussed what needed to happen to 'shrink' the avoidant part and expand the 'healthy' or 'wise' supervisee part. By considering the respective sizes of different parts, they could decide which part to 'interview' or which part to temporarily 'banish' from the supervision session.

The examples provided within this chapter are but a 'toe in the water' of what is possible through chair work. Further examples include

- Understanding strong counter-transference reactions to a client
- Rehearsing conversations with a client
- Taking on the role of negative automatic thoughts and 'countering' this with rational responses
- Empty chair work with a critical former supervisor

Further considerations

A survey of CBT therapists found that many did not use chair work, and those who did lacked confidence in this method (Pugh et al., 2021). Aside from training opportunities, chair work has the potential to generate high levels of effect (e.g. anger, sadness); therefore, some therapists (e.g. those high in experiential avoidance) may fear eliciting this from their clients or within themselves (Presley et al., 2023). Meta-supervision should be used to address any fears or concerns supervisors might have about using chair work.

Questions for meta-supervision

I have never done any training in chair work, should I delay introducing it until I understand it better?

I'd like to see it demonstrated before I use it in supervision. Could we try it out within meta-supervision?

Chapter summary

- Chair work involves using multiple chairs in therapy or supervision to embody different perspectives.
- It creates distance and flexibility, allowing exploration of beliefs, emotions and behaviours that might be linked to supervisee avoidance or problems within therapy.
- It can help by enhancing empathy for clients, understanding avoidance behaviours, addressing strong countertransference reactions or rehearsing difficult conversations.
- Chair work helps to normalise self-multiplicity (being 'in two minds') and naming different parts of the self, and it offers experiential alternatives to standard CBT interventions (e.g. cost-benefit analysis, thought records).

Recommended reading

Pugh, M. (2019). A little less talk, a little more action: A dialogical approach to cognitive therapy. *The Cognitive Behaviour Therapist*, 12, e47.

Afterword

The intention of this book was to champion active methods within supervision, highlighting their integral role within therapist skill development. Research on routine supervisory practices indicates that supervision often relies on case discussion, calling into question the degree to which supervisors can confidently assess the skills of their supervisees. In Chapter 2, I summarised the main supervisor behaviours that seem most likely to create an optimal learning environment for supervisees:

- Helping the supervisee to develop their clinical skills
- Displaying cultural awareness and humility
- Offering regular and fair feedback
- Addressing difficulties within the relationship when they arise
- Being warm and open and inviting feedback on the effectiveness of supervision sessions

The methods outlined in parts two and three of the book help to demonstrate specific ways in which CBT supervisors can 'embody' these behaviours. There are, of course, other active methods that have not been discussed, and supervisors are encouraged to see this book as a starting point rather than a finite list of methods, a means of igniting their passion for a more active and immersive approach to the supervision they provide.

I have also proposed that there are wider 'systemic' factors that shape the beliefs and behaviours of supervisors – the culture of what is deemed normal and acceptable practices within CBT as a whole and the context, the environment in which therapy and supervision take place. Here, I outline several considerations for CBT supervisors, researchers and policy makers in terms of the factors that might shape supervision in years to come.

Technology and supervision

The COVID-19 pandemic saw most therapists needing to use online platforms to conduct therapy sessions, and it quickly became apparent how useful these could be in terms of addressing common barriers to client engagement. Several years

DOI: 10.4324/9781003590620-24

later, the popularity of online working has not declined; therefore, recording and sharing videos with one's supervisor should, in theory, be much simpler. Technology also has the potential to provide more sophisticated means of tracking therapist outcomes and therefore therapist and supervisor drift. This is likely to have mixed reception. On the one hand, this makes it easier to capture problematic patterns; on the other hand, some might feel that this is another level of micro-management that pushes therapists out of the NHS and into private practice.

Supporting supervisee wellbeing

The focus of most of the chapters in this book has been geared towards enhancing supervisee learning, with a recognition that supervisees also need to feel safe enough to grow within the supervisory relationship. For supervisors, there is also a need to consider how they attend to the restorative component of supervision. That said, there is a fine line we must tread as supervisors whereby we respect the boundaries of the supervisory relationship and not fall into the trap of becoming a therapist to our supervisees. SP/SR and the use of supervision satisfaction scales such as the LASS help to ensure that there is a balance between supervisee safety and growth as a therapist.

It would seem that for psychological therapists, irrespective of their therapeutic modality, there is a high risk of burnout. This is characterised by emotional exhaustion, depersonalisation and a diminishing sense of personal achievement (Maslach & Jackson, 1981). Burnt out therapists often become (understandably) less effective, perhaps zoning out during therapy sessions or feeling mentally defeated by their client's interpersonal style or extensive list of problems. They might also struggle to feel empathy or compassion towards their clients because of these factors, and in these situations, supervision will play a crucial role in supporting them to identify and work through the early warning signs of burnout.

For therapists with autism or ADHD there are additional daily challenges (e.g. processing information, dealing with systems that are designed for the neurotypical), whilst therapists from ethnic minority backgrounds can face an endless stream of microaggressions from both clients and colleagues. With many CBT therapists working in high-pressure environments, how do supervisors make the time to support their supervisees whilst retaining a focus on client outcomes and adherence to CBT principles and practices?

I would argue that the Pre-Supervision Questionnaire that features in this book can play a central role in placing these issues at the heart of supervisory discussions and activities. In addition to this, formulation of therapist beliefs, emotions and behaviours is as important as the formulations that we create for our clients; therefore, supervisors should hold in mind the parallel processes of therapy and supervisory relationships.

Access to meta-supervision (MS)

Given that one of the central aims of supervision is to monitor treatment adherence, therapist competence and ethical practice (Rakovshik et al., 2016) it is imperative that those monitoring this (supervisors) are, to some degree, monitored themselves to ensure that the supervision they provide achieves these objectives (Loades & Armstrong, 2016; Milne et al., 2011). There is a need to gauge how often MS is accessed in routine supervisory practice, with earlier research indicating that it is rarely available (e.g. Townend et al., 2002 found that 53% of BABCP accredited therapists did not receive MS). Beyond this we need to understand who is best placed to provide this? Should it be conducted as a separate activity from standard supervision? What level of experience is required for one to be an effective meta-supervisor?

Supervisor training

Supervisor training is currently optional, and when it is available, it varies in length, content and whether or not it includes a formal assessment of skills (Taylor et al., 2012). Unless one chooses to become an accredited supervisor, annual Continuing Professional Development may not be on the radar for many supervisors, meaning that their skills are prone to decay or arrested development. If we truly value supervision, then we should consider the degree to which we invest in training, both at the start of one's journey in this role and throughout their career as a supervisor. Clearly, training costs money, and therefore we need to view this as an employer's responsibility to support their staff, rather than it always falling on the individual to foot the bill.

Future research

The ideas presented within this book can be seen as sitting at various points between theory and evidence-based practice. We have very well-established active methods such as reviewing live material and promising developments such as Deliberate Practice that require testing within a CBT population. There are also several scales, such as the Alignment to CBT scale (Appendix 5) and the BASS-12 (Appendix 4), which need to be tested for construct validity. We also need to understand supervisor confidence in addressing issues such as role transition and in using more novel methods such as chair work. In summary, there is a lot that we still need to find out about supervision in terms of its mechanisms of change and how we can help supervisors to feel enthused enough to take it to even higher levels than we see at present.

Appendix 1

Active methods FAQs

Q. What constitutes an active method within supervision?

A. As discussed in Chapter 2, there is a continuum of 'activeness' that depends on two things – how involved the supervisee is and how evocative and immersive the method is. When the supervisor models an intervention, the supervisee remains passive, however if they then switch roles and the supervisee replicates what they have observed, the exercise because more evocative and immersive. In essence rather than thinking that a method is active or inactive, it is important to consider it a sliding scale.

Q. My supervisee is reluctant to engage in active methods, what should I do in this scenario?

A. It would be useful to explore their previous experiences of supervision and whether or not this included active methods (this could be done using the pre-supervision questionnaire). Perhaps they have had a bad experience where they felt criticised or humiliated. It would also be helpful to determine if they understand the rationale for active methods. One way around reluctance is to treat the use of active methods as a behavioural experiment. What do they think will happen? What evidence will show if this comes true? What actually happened? What can they learn from the experience?

Q. I don't feel confident enough to use active methods within supervision. What would be the best starting point?

A. It is important for you to understand what the barrier is and how you might overcome this. Is it due to a lack of exposure to active methods in your own supervision and therefore a need to see how it is done? You could ask your meta-supervisor (if you have access to one) to model a specific method or build them into SoS on a regular basis. Perhaps it is due to your own therapist schemas such as demanding standards. The fear of not doing it perfectly gets in the way of even attempting it due to the belief that one will be judged harshly by the supervisee.

Q. Can I insist on using active methods is a supervisee is reluctant or unwilling?

A. There are certain active methods that are unavoidable for supervisees during training such as showing video recordings. With qualified therapists, there is often less of a mandate and those in PP can usually vote with their feet if they don't like what you are offering. You could specify within your contract that active methods are a non-negotiable part of being their supervisor. Ultimately, whilst you cannot make the supervisee engage in active methods, you can make the case that in not doing so, you unable to fulfil all of your normative and formative duties and on this basis, and suggest that the supervisee find an alternative supervisor.

Q. How do I know if my supervision sessions are active enough?

A. It is helpful to hold in mind Kolb's learning cycle during each supervision session and to consider if you are getting the supervisee to plan, experience, observe and reflect

There are two frameworks that can help us to monitor how active we are as supervisors. Firstly, we can consider if we are following the ten steps outlined by Gordon (2012). Secondly, we can formally audit our supervisory practice at regular intervals. For example, We can use the questionnaire in Chapter 2 or record supervision sessions and formally rate them using a tool such as the SAGE or Short SAGE (Milne et al., 2011; Reiser et al., 2018) within Supervision of Supervision.

Appendix 2

CBT supervisee self-assessment checklist

This handout is designed to help you to consider some clear steps that you can take to be as effective a supervisee as possible. Being an effective supervisee applies as much to qualified therapists as it does to trainees. By following the steps below, you will be able to maximise your learning in supervision and make it a more enjoyable experience.

1 Embrace the Collaborative Nature of CBT Supervision
Whenever possible, prepare your supervision questions in advance – this saves time when setting the agenda.
Try to align your supervision question with a SMART goal for that supervision session.
Reflective Questions:
Do I help shape the supervision agenda?
Am I using supervision time effectively?
Do I understand the structure and goals of CBT supervision?

2 Get Off to a Good Start
Discuss past supervision experiences during contracting.
Clarify expectations and preferences with your supervisor.
Reflective Questions:
Have I shared my supervision history and preferences?
Do I understand how my supervisor's style aligns with mine?

3 Prepare for Each Supervision Session
Bring client formulations and other relevant material (e.g. scores on outcome measures).
Identify specific supervision questions beforehand.
Consider using a preparation worksheets to help refine your questions (e.g. Padesky's supervision consultation worksheet).
Reflective Questions:
Do I come prepared with materials and questions?
Am I using tools to structure my supervision input?

4 Set and Review Supervision Goals
Define clear learning goals based on strengths and weaknesses.

Review goals regularly with your supervisor.
Reflective Questions:
Have I set meaningful goals for supervision?
Do I revisit and revise these goals periodically?

5 Accept Constructive Criticism
Invite feedback through role-play or session recordings.
Differentiate between criticism of your work and criticism of you as a person.
Reflective Questions:
Am I open to feedback regardless of my experience level?
Do I seek opportunities to receive constructive input?

6 Manage Avoidance and Discomfort
Notice your emotional responses to supervision tasks.
Challenge your urge to avoid or to use safety behaviors.
Reflective Questions:
Do I avoid tasks that make me uncomfortable?
Can I identify and challenge my predictions and urges?

7 Raise Concerns and Evaluate Supervision
Discuss supervision content and style openly.
Use feedback tools (e.g. satisfaction rating scales).
Reflective Questions:
Do I feel safe raising concerns with my supervisor?
Are we evaluating the usefulness of supervision together?

Appendix 3

Considerations for group supervision

Whilst most of the content in this book has been applied to a dyadic format of supervision (e.g. one to one), it is recognised that most therapists will have supervision in a group context at some stage in their career. For that reason, some adjustments to active methods are considered here where there are two or more supervisees present.

Wearing different hats for different supervisees

The different supervision questions that are brought by each group member is likely to mean that as a supervisor, you are regularly moving between each of the three functions within one session. For example, an ethical query from one supervisee will require a normative focus, whilst a question about how to treat worries in GAD will shift to a formative focus. There might also be a supervisee who is feeling discouraged from a client dropping out of treatment and engaging in self-blame and rumination thus requiring a restorative focus.

Retaining the normative and formative functions

Group supervision is at risk of becoming dominated by case discussion. Firstly, formats such as peer supervision where there is no one 'in charge' can become a competition for who can shout the loudest or whose opinion is more impressive. Secondly, due to time constraints (individuals typically have less time to present their cases in a group compared to one to one supervision), showing videos or role-play exercises can be considered to be time and labour intensive by group members. It is recommended that individuals complete the Pre-supervision questionnaire in Chapter 10 and share their summary with peers in the contracting phase of peer supervision to that learning styles are taken into account.

When supervisees are at different IDM Stages

Group supervision throws up many challenges, not least the fact that due to different professional backgrounds, trainees will start their CBT training at different levels across all skill domains. These differences are usually more pronounced amongst qualified therapists. For example, some supervisors might assume that two supervisees who have been qualified for the same period of time (e.g. three years) will be at the same 'global' IDM level.

Due to reasons already covered in the chapter, this is unlikely to be the case and therefore, it underscores the importance of meeting with group members separately during the contracting stage to determine strengths and weaknesses.

Supervisors can then 'refresh' their knowledge of their supervision group by quickly viewing each member's IDM Snapshot before each session.

When there are more than two people peddling!

The tandem bike analogy introduced in Chapter 9 fits well when there is just one supervisee but what happens when you are supervising a group? There are several immediate challenges when thinking about managing more than one persons' supervision journey. Firstly, there is usually less time to focus on each group member (e.g. 30 minutes each compared to a full hour or longer in one to one supervision). Secondly, not all trainees arrive with an equal level of skills (e.g. some have more CBT specific knowledge and skills and some have better interpersonal skills). Thirdly, there might be considerable variation in the context in which they are practising CBT (e.g. Primary Care, Prisons, PP). Consequently, the supervisor has to consider many variables when trying to ensure that the journey is not to quick or slow and that it does not take too many detours because of the needs of some group members.

Addressing stylistic differences

When supervising trainees, it is highly likely that their previous professional role will serve as a template for how they interact within supervision. For example, those who have been person-centred counsellors might be used to supervision as being a more open-ended personal reflective space. In contrast, PWP's might expect a more 'outcomes orientated' discussion, presenting extensive information on Psychometric scores. It is important to understand the default 'supervision schema' for each group member and socialise them to the structure every session. This might involve regularly pausing them to reflect on the function of a given behaviour. Setting and returning to the agenda, together with refining their supervision question will help to instil this approach.

Adapting the PSQ for group supervision

The PSQ specifically asks if there are any personal factors that the supervisee would not want to be discussed in a group format. This helps the supervisor to be alert to salient aspects that can be shared during discussions and those where the supervisee is less comfortable about other group members. Whilst it can be tempting to frame all avoidance as problematic and therefore a target for change, supervisors should consider the function of the behaviour rather than the form. For example, a supervisee might feel reluctant to share video recordings in front of other group members and requests that they be exempt from this. Another supervisee is in the process of coming to terms with their sexuality and is not yet 'out'. Whilst they have written this on the PSQ for their supervisor to be aware of, they do not wish for other group members to know. In the first example, the supervisor should encourage the supervisee to work towards sharing recordings as this is a core component of supervision however, in the second example, the supervisor should respect the wishes of the supervisees rather than pressurising them to share their sexuality with the group.

Sensitively addressing drift in front of other supervisees

Shining a light on therapist drift can be a shaming experience if the supervisee feels that the supervisor has singled them out (e.g. to make an example of them). In a group context, the supervisor can ask all members to fill out the scales mentioned earlier and have more general discussions about fears, doubts and avoidance. The supervisor can also normalise drift and share their own experiences of when they have drifted or have had the temptation to drift, There are times when the supervisor needs to address drift such as if it is causing significant problems in the progress of their client. The supervisor might choose to email or phone to supervisee outside of the group session if they need to address ethical concerns or serious concerns about the competence of the supervisee.ww

Appendix 4

Beliefs about Supervision Scale (BASS-12)

The Beliefs about Supervision Scale (BASS-12) is a twelve-item reflective tool that has been developed with the intention of helping supervisors and supervisees to reflect upon various attitudes towards aspects of CBT supervision (Roscoe, 2026). At this point in time, the BASS-12 has not undergone any form of official validation as a measure. Items have been generated by sending a list to a small number of highly experienced supervisors. It contains statements that reveal certain assumptions about supervision, the role of a supervisor and their relationship with their supervisees. Items were deleted or added based on the feedback from these supervisors.

Whilst there are no right or wrong answers per se, there might be several unintended consequences of holding some of these attitudes tightly. For example, believing strongly that Self-Practice/Self-Reflection (SP/SR) has no place in supervision could mean that a supervisor misses out on many opportunities to help their supervisees tap into this avenue of skill building.

For each statement please allocate a score based on the strength to which you agree with what is written.

0 – Completely Disagree
1 – Mostly Disagree
2 – Disagree Slightly
3 – Neutral
4– Slightly Agree
5 – Mostly Agree
6 – Completely Agree

Belief	*Score 0–6 for each item*
1 Supervision is about developing technical skills not discussing personal matters 2 Self-Practice/Self Reflection has no place in supervision 3 Supervision of Supervision is unnecessary 4 Supervision models are restrictive and stifle creativity	

(Continued)

(Continued)

Belief	*Score 0–6 for each item*
5 Supervisory experience and intuition are more helpful than supervision models	
6 It is not necessary to formally rate the skills of qualified supervisees	
7 It is unnecessary to change the style of supervision for trainees and qualified clinicians	
8 Role-play and skills practice make people feel too uncomfortable	
9 It would be terrible to experience a rupture within supervision	
10 It is too anxiety provoking to challenge the ethical practice of a supervisee	
11 It is unnecessary to adapt one's supervision style according to the supervisee's cultural background	
12 Supervisees should always take the advice of the supervisor about formulations and interventions	

Appendix 5

Alignment to CBT scale (Roscoe, 2023b)

The scale has not been subject to a research trial and is based largely on observations of trainees across multiple cohorts in a single CBT training site. The scale is intended to aid self-reflection rather than to determine a 'cut-off score' for suitability.

The scale has five sections:

1 Receptiveness to structure
2 Attitudes towards measurement
3 Responsibility for change
4 Use of sessions
5 Capacity for tolerating distress

Whilst there is no 'cut-off' score, the more that you identify with the questions, the more suited you might be to CBT as a career. Score each item based on the following:

0 – Not at all like me
1 – A little like me
2 – Quite like me
3 – Moderately like me
4 – Mostly like me
5 – Very much like me

Personal characteristic	*Score 0–5*
Receptiveness to structure	
1 I like sessions to be focused on specific problems rather than talking about whatever is on the clients mind that day 2 I think it is important for clients to be set homework tasks between sessions 3 It is important that sessions do not over-run, even if this means interrupting a client	

(Continued)

(Continued)

Personal characteristic	*Score 0–5*
Attitudes towards measurement	
4 It is important to have an objective measure of the effectiveness of therapy and questionnaires are helpful in achieving this 5 Diagnostic classification helps to pinpoint formulation and treatment plans 6 I like to follow evidence-based treatment plans rather than using my intuition about what the client needs from me	
Responsibility for change	
7 I do not have to have all the answers to my clients' problems to be of help to them 8 I can refrain from sharing my own personal experiences with clients 9 I do not try to persuade clients of the need to change	
Use of sessions	
10 I like to be active during therapy sessions rather than simply talking about a client's difficulties 11 I would enjoy going out into the community and helping clients to face their fears 12 I like being creative in how I help clients to make sense of their difficulties and to change their thinking and behaviour	
Capacity for tolerating distress	
13 I recognise that helping clients to change involves them facing difficult thoughts, emotions, memories and bodily sensations 14 I am willing to encourage clients to talk about aversive life experiences such as rape, sexual abuse, or torture to help them process the memories 15 I can tolerate my own anxiety about the outcome of various interventions 16 I can help to contain the client if they become distressed or dissociated during therapy sessions	

Appendix 6

Supervisee Summary Record

Supervisee Summary Record

Supervisee Initials ____
Frequency of Supervision __________
Level of CBT Training ____________
Length of time qualified _________
Approximate Overall IDM Level __________

Current Goals for Supervision:

Date of next review:

Salient information captured within the PSQ

Key strengths	
Key areas for development	
Preferred methods within supervision	
Least favourite methods within supervision	
Salient background information	
Potential therapy-interfering beliefs and behaviours	
Potential supervision-interfering beliefs and behaviours	

IDM Snapshot (adapted to fit specifically with CBT)

Supervisee Initials	
Frequency of Supervision	
Level of CBT Training/Status	
Length of time qualified	
Approximate Overall IDM Level	
Specific IDM Skill Domains Ratings (1, 2, 3 or 3i)	

(Continued)

(Continued)

Assessment Skills	
Case Conceptualisation Skills	
Session Structure	
Skilful application of techniques (e.g. CBT Interventions)	
Treatment Planning	
Interpersonal Skills	
Cultural Competence	
Understanding of Ethics	
Style/Stance (Alignment to CBT)	

References

American Psychiatric Association. (2013). *Diagnostic and statistical manual of mental disorders* (5th ed).

Armstrong, P. V., & Freeston, M. H. (2006). Conceptualising and formulating cognitive therapy supervision. In Tarrier, N. (Ed.) *Case formulation in cognitive behaviour therapy* (pp. 349–371). Routledge/Taylor & Francis Group.

BABCP. (2025). *Minimum training standards*. Bury: British Association for Behavioural & Cognitive Psychotherapies.

Barkham, M., De Jong, K., Delgadillo, J., & Lutz, W. (2023). Routine outcome monitoring (ROM) and feedback: Research review and recommendations. *Psychotherapy Research*, 33(7), 841–855.

Barton, S., & Armstrong, P. (2018). *CBT for depression: An integrated approach*. SAGE.

Bearman, S. K., Schneiderman, R. L., & Zoloth, E. (2017). Building an evidence base for effective supervision practices: An analogue experiment of supervision to increase EBT fidelity. *Administration and Policy in Mental Health and Mental Health Services Research*, 44, 293–307.

Beaumont, E., & Hollins Martin, C. J. (2013). Using compassionate mind training as a resource in EMDR: A case study. *Journal of EMDR Practice and Research*, 7(4), 186–199.

Beck, A. (2016). *Transcultural cognitive behavioural therapy for anxiety and depression: A practical guide*. Routledge. https://doi.org/10.4324/9781315707419

Beck, A. T., Rush, A. J., Shaw, B. F., & Emery, G. (1979). *Cognitive therapy of depression*. Guilford Press.

Beck, J. S. (1995). *Cognitive therapy: Basics and beyond* (No. Sirsi). Guilford Press.

Beinart, H. (2014). Building and sustaining the supervisory relationship. In Watkins Jr, C. E. & Milne, D. L. (Eds.) *The Wiley international handbook of clinical supervision*. John Wiley & Sons.

Bell, T., Montague, J., Elander, J., & Gilbert, P. (2020). 'A definite feel-it moment': Embodiment, externalisation and emotion during chair-work in compassion-focused therapy. *Counselling and Psychotherapy Research*, 20(1), 143–153.

Bennett-Levy, J. (2006). Therapist skills: A cognitive model of their acquisition and refinement. *Behavioural and Cognitive Psychotherapy*, 34, 57–78.

Bennett-Levy, J. (2019). Why therapists should walk the talk: The theoretical and empirical case for personal practice in therapist training and professional development. *Journal of Behavior Therapy and Experimental Psychiatry*, 62, 133–145. https://doi.org/10.1016/j.jbtep.2018.08.004

Bennett-Levy, J., & Beedie, A. (2007). The ups and downs of cognitive therapy training: What happens to trainees' perception of their competence during a cognitive therapy training course? *Behavioural and Cognitive Psychotherapy*, 35(1), 61–75.

Bennett-Levy, J., & Finlay-Jones, A. (2018). The role of personal practice in therapist skill development: A model to guide therapists, educators, supervisors and researchers. *Cognitive Behaviour Therapy*, 47(3), 185–205.

Bennett-Levy, J., McManus, F., Westling, B. E., & Fennell, M. (2009). Acquiring and refining CBT skills and competencies: Which training methods are perceived to be most effective? *Behavioural and cognitive psychotherapy*, 37(5), 571–583.

Bennett-Levy, J., Thwaites, R., Haarhoff, B., & Perry, H. (2014). *Experiencing CBT from the inside out: A self-practice/self-reflection workbook for therapists*. Guilford Press.

Bennett-Levy, J., Turner, F., Beaty, T., Smith, M., Paterson, B., & Farmer, S. (2001). The value of self-practice of cognitive therapy techniques and self-reflection in the training of cognitive therapists. *Behavioural and Cognitive Psychotherapy*, 29(2), 203–220. https://doi.org/10.1017/S1352465801002077

Bernard, J. M., & Goodyear, R. K. (2014). *Fundamentals of clinical supervision*. Allyn & Bacon.

Birdsey, N. (2020). Integrating CBT and CFT within a case formulation approach to reduce depression and anxiety in an older adult with a complex mental and physical health history: A single case study. *The Cognitive Behaviour Therapist*, 13, e41.

Black, L. L., & Stone, D. (2005). Expanding the definition of privilege: The concept of social privilege. *Journal of Multicultural Counseling and Development*, 33(4), 243–255.

Blackburn, I. M., James, I. A., Milne, D. L., Reichelt, F. K., Garland, A., Baker, C., & Claydon, A. (2001). *Cognitive therapy scale-revised (CTS-R)*. Newcastle Cognitive and Behavioural Therapies Centre.

Bordin, E. S. (1983). A working alliance based model of supervision. *The Counseling Psychologist*, 11(1), 35–42. https://doi.org/10.1177/0011000083111007

Boswell, J. F., & Constantino, M. J. (2021). *Deliberate practice in cognitive behavioural therapy*. American Psychological Association.

Bream, V., Challacombe, F., Palmer, A., & Salkovskis, P. (2017). *Cognitive behaviour therapy for obsessive-compulsive disorder*. Oxford University Press.

Brosan, L., Reynolds, S., & Moore, R. G. (2008). Self-evaluation of cognitive therapy performance: Do therapists know how competent they are? *Behavioural and Cognitive Psychotherapy*, 36(5), 581–587.

Bruun, M. K. (2023). 'A factory of therapy': Accountability and the monitoring of psychological therapy in IAPT. *Anthropology & Medicine*, 30(4), 313–329.

Buchanan, N. T. (2020). Salient circles diagrams: Making intersectional identities, privilege, power, and marginalization visible. *Women & Therapy*, 43(3–4), 400–404.

Burnham, J. (2012). Developments in social GRRRAAACCEEESSS: Visible-invisible and voiced-unvoiced. In Krause, I.-B. (Ed.) *Culture and reflexivity in systemic psychotherapy: Mutual perspectives* (pp. 139–160). Karnac Books Ltd.

Butler, A. C., Chapman, J. E., Forman, E. M., & Beck, A. T. (2006). The empirical status of cognitive-behavioral therapy: A review of metaanalyses. *Clinical Psychology Review*, 26(1), 17–31. https://doi.org/10.1016/j.cpr.2005.07.003

Butler, G., Fennell, M., & Hackmann, A. (2010). *Cognitive-behavioral therapy for anxiety disorders: Mastering clinical challenges*. Guilford Press.

Campbell-Lee, D., Barton, S., & Armstrong, P. (2024). Higher-order CBT skills: Are there differences in meta-competence between trainee and experienced therapists? *The Cognitive Behaviour Therapist*, 17, e7.

Chowdhury, S. S., Churchard, A., Lawton, L., Malik, Z., Thwaites, R., & Clements, H. (2025). A novel self-practice/self-reflection programme for CBT therapists from minoritised ethnic backgrounds: A multiple baselines single case experimental study. *The Cognitive Behaviour Therapist*, 18, e15.

Clark, D. M. (1986). A cognitive approach to panic. *Behaviour Research and Therapy*, 24(4), 461–470.

Clark, D. M. (2011). Implementing NICE guidelines for the psychological treatment of depression and anxiety disorders: The IAPT experience. *International Review of Psychiatry*, 23(4), 318–327.

Clements-Hickman, A. L., & Harris, K. R. (2024). Deliberate practice for psychotherapy skills: Recommendations and implications based on the state of the science. *Professional Psychology: Research and Practice*, 55(6), 563–572

Clohessy, S. (2019). *The supervisory relationship and contracting*. Oxford Cognitive Therapy Centre, CPD Event, 25 November.

Corrie, S., & Lane, D. A. (2016). Supporting the supervisor: Organizing professional development to enhance practice. *The Cognitive Behaviour Therapist*, 9, e23.

Crenshaw, K. (1989). Demarginalizing the intersection of race and sex: A Black feminist critique of antidiscrimination doctrine, feminist theory and antiracist politics. *University of Chicago Legal Form*, 140(1), 139–167.

Daley, J., Hale, L., & Patton, B. (2022). Clinical psychology trainees' experiences of following a specialised cognitive behavioural therapy (CBT) pathway accredited by the British Association of Behavioural and Cognitive Psychotherapies (BABCP): A pilot evaluation. *Clinical Psychology Forum*, 349, 28–34.

Davidson, K. (2008). *Cognitive therapy for personality disorders: A guide for clinicians*. Routledge.

Davis, M. L., Thwaites, R., Freeston, M. H., & Bennett-Levy, J. (2015). A measurable impact of a self-practice/self-reflection programme on the therapeutic skills of experienced cognitive-behavioural therapists. *Clinical Psychology & Psychotherapy*, 22(2), 176–184. https://doi.org/10.1002/cpp.1884

Deacon, B. J., Farrell, N. R., Kemp, J. J., Dixon, L. J., Sy, J. T., Zhang, A. R., & McGrath, P. B. (2013). Assessing therapist reservations about exposure therapy for anxiety disorders: The therapist beliefs about exposure scale. *Journal of Anxiety Disorders*, 27, 772–780. https://doi.org/10.1016/j.janxdis.2013.04.006

Delgadillo, J., Deisenhofer, A. K., Probst, T., Shimokawa, K., Lambert, M. J., & Kleinstäuber, M. (2022). Progress feedback narrows the gap between more and less effective therapists: A therapist effects meta-analysis of clinical trials. *Journal of Consulting and Clinical Psychology*, 90(7), 559.

De Stefano, J., Hutman, H., & Gazzola, N. (2017). Putting on the face: A qualitative study of power dynamics in clinical supervision. *The Clinical Supervisor*, 36(2), 223–240.

D'Souza Walsh, K., Davies, L., Pluckwell, H., Huffinley, H., & Waller, G. (2019). Alliance, technique, both, or more? Clinicians' views on what works in cognitive-behavioral therapy for eating disorders. *International Journal of Eating Disorders*, 52(3), 278–282. https://doi.org/10.1002/eat.23033

Ehlers, A., & Clark, D. M. (2000). A cognitive model of posttraumatic stress disorder. *Behaviour Research and Therapy*, 38, 319–345.

Ellis, M. V., Berger, L., Hanus, A. E., Ayala, E. E., Swords, B. A., & Siembor, M. (2014). Inadequate and harmful clinical supervision: Testing a revised framework and assessing occurrence. *The Counseling Psychologist*, 42(4), 434–472.

Ericsson, K. A., Krampe, R. T., & Tesch-Römer, C. (1993). The role of deliberate practice in the acquisition of expert performance. *Psychological Review*, 100(3), 363.

Faheem, A. (2023). 'It's been quite a poor show' – exploring whether practitioners working for Improving Access to Psychological Therapies (IAPT) services are culturally competent to deal with the needs of Black, Asian and Minority Ethnic (BAME) communities. *The Cognitive Behaviour Therapist*, 16, E6. https://doi.org/10.1017/S1754470X22000642

Fairburn, C. G. (2008). *Cognitive behavior therapy and eating disorders*. Guilford Press.

Fennell, M. J. (1997). Low self-esteem: A cognitive perspective. *Behavioural and Cognitive Psychotherapy*, 25(1), 1–26.

Foa, E. B., Kozak, M. J., Salkovskis, P. M., Coles, M. E., & Amir, N. (1998). The validation of a new obsessive–compulsive disorder scale: The obsessive–compulsive inventory. *Psychological Assessment*, 10(3), 206.

Freeston, M. H., Thwaites, R., & Bennett-Levy, J. (2019). 'Courses for horses': Designing, adapting and implementing self practice/self-reflection programmes. *The Cognitive Behaviour Therapist*, 12, e28.

Gonsalvez, C. J., Brockman, R., & Hill, H. R. (2016). Video feedback in CBT supervision: Review and illustration of two specific techniques. *The Cognitive Behaviour Therapist*, 9, e24.

Gordon, P. K. (2012). Ten steps to cognitive behavioural supervision. *The Cognitive Behaviour Therapist*, 5.

Grant, A., Townend, M., & Sloan, G. (2008). The transfer of CBT education from classroom to work setting: Getting it right or wasting the opportunities? *The Cognitive Behaviour Therapist*, 1, 27–44.

Haarhoff, B., Thwaites, R., & Bennett-Levy, J. (2015). Engagement with self-practice/self-reflection as a professional development activity: The role of therapist beliefs. *Australian Psychologist*, 50(5), 322–328.

Haarhoff, B. A. (2006). The importance of identifying and understanding therapist schema in cognitive therapy training and supervision. *New Zealand Journal of Psychology*, 35, 126–131.

Haddock, G., Devane, S., Bradshaw, T., McGovern, J., Tarrier, N., Kinderman, P., . . . & Harris, N. (2001). An investigation into the psychometric properties of the cognitive therapy scale for psychosis (CTS-Psy). *Behavioural and Cognitive Psychotherapy*, 29(2), 221–233.

Harper, K., Bhutani, G., Rao, A. S., & Clarke, J. (2020). Wellbeing matters in IAPT practitioners: Identity vs system. *International Journal of Stress Prevention and Wellbeing*, 4(4), 1–12.

Haug, T., Nordgreen, T., Öst, L. G., Tangen, T., Kvale, G., Hovland, O. J., . . . & Havik, O. E. (2016). Working alliance and competence as predictors of outcome in cognitive behavioral therapy for social anxiety and panic disorder in adults. *Behaviour Research and Therapy*, 77, 40–51.

Hawkins, P., & Shohet, R. (2000). *Supervision in the helping professions*. Open University Press.

Henretty, J. R., & Levitt, H. M. (2010). The role of therapist self-disclosure in psychotherapy: A qualitative review. *Clinical Psychology Review*, 30(1), 63–77.

Hoffman, M. A., Hill, C. E., Holmes, S. E., & Freitas, G. F. (2005). Supervisor perspective on the process and outcome of giving easy, difficult, or no feedback to supervisees. *Journal of Counseling Psychology*, 52(1), 3.

Holloway, E. (1995). *Clinical supervision: A systems approach*. Sage.

Hope, T. (2010) Ethics. In Mueller, M., Kennerley, H., McManus, F. & Westbrook, D. (Eds.) *Oxford guide to surviving as a CBT therapist*. Oxford University Press.

James, I. A., Milne, D., & Morse, R. (2008). Microskills of clinical supervision: Scaffolding skills. *Journal of Cognitive Psychotherapy*, 22(1), 29.

Johnston, L. H., & Milne, D. L. (2012). How do supervisee's learn during supervision? A grounded theory study of the perceived developmental process. *The Cognitive Behaviour Therapist*, 5, 1–23.

Katzow, A. W., & Safran, J. D. (2010). Recognizing and resolving ruptures in the therapeutic alliance. In Gilbert, P. & Leahy, R. (Eds.) *The therapeutic relationship in the cognitive behavioral psychotherapies* (pp. 106–121). Routledge.

Kazantzis, N. (2003). Therapist competence in cognitive-behavioural therapies: Review of the contemporary empirical evidence. *Behaviour Change*, 20(1), 1–12.

Kendall, P. C., & Frank, H. E. (2018). Implementing evidence-based treatment protocols: Flexibility within fidelity. *Clinical Psychology: Science and Practice*, 25(4), 40.

Kolb, D. A. (1984). *Experiential learning: Experience as the source of learning and development.* Prentice Hall.

Koshy, E., Koshy, V., & Waterman, H. (2011). *Action research in healthcare.* SAGE Publications Ltd.

Kroenke, K., Spitzer, R. L., & Williams, J. B. (2001). The PHQ-9: Validity of a brief depression severity measure. *Journal of General Internal Medicine*, 16(9), 606–613.

Ladany, N., Mori, Y., & Mehr, K. E. (2013). Effective and ineffective supervision. *The Counseling Psychologist*, 41, 28–47.

Laville, A., Chandar, A. M., Meek, N., & Vialls, E. (2025). Embedding inclusive principles within your CBT practice: Working with autism, gender identity, and sexual orientation. In Roscoe, J. (Ed.) *Becoming a CBT therapist: Thriving in training and beyond* (pp. 140–151). Routledge.

Leahy, R. (2001). *Overcoming resistance in cognitive therapy.* Guilford Press.

Leahy, R. L. (2002). A model of emotional schemas. *Cognitive and Behavioral Practice*, 9(3), 177–190.

Leahy, R. L. (2008). The therapeutic relationship in cognitive-behavioral therapy. *Behavioural and Cognitive Psychotherapy*, 36(6), 769–777.

Leahy, R. L. (2018). *The jealousy cure: Learn to trust, overcome possessiveness, and save your relationship.* New Harbinger Publications.

Ledley, D. R., Marx, B. P., & Heimberg, R. G. (2011). *Making cognitive-behavioral therapy work: Clinical process for new practitioners.* Guilford Press.

Lee, J. A., Neimeyer, G. J., & Rice, K. G. (2013). The relationship between therapist epistemology, therapy style, working alliance, and interventions use. *American Journal of Psychotherapy*, 67, 323–345.

Lewis, M. (2024). An exploration of the ways in which person-centered counselors' diagnoses of attention-deficit/hyperactivity disorder (ADHD) can challenge or support their practice. *Person-Centered & Experiential Psychotherapies*, 23(2), 203–221.

Liese, B. S., & Beck, J. S. (1997). Cognitive therapy supervision. In Watkins Jr., C. E. (Ed.) *Handbook of psychotherapy supervision* (pp. 114–133). John Wiley & Sons, Inc.

Limper-Menapace, J. (2025). Managing as a trainee with lived experience of mental health difficulties. In Roscoe, J. (Ed.), *Becoming a CBT therapist: Thriving in training and beyond* (pp. 140–151). Routledge.

Liness, S., Beale, S., Lea, S., Byrne, S., Hirsch, C. R., & Clark, D. M. (2019). The sustained effects of CBT training on therapist competence and patient outcomes. *Cognitive Therapy and Research*, 43, 631–641.

Liness, S., Lea, S., Nestler, S., Parker, H., & Clark, D. M. (2017). What IAPT CBT high-intensity trainees do after training. *Behavioural and Cognitive Psychotherapy*, 45(1), 16–30.

Loades, M. E., & Armstrong, P. (2016). The challenge of training supervisors to use direct assessments of clinical competence in CBT consistently: A systematic review and exploratory training study. *The Cognitive Behaviour Therapist*, 9, e27.

Mahon, D. (2023). A scoping review of deliberate practice in the acquisition of therapeutic skills and practices. *Counselling and Psychotherapy Research*, 23(4), 965–981.

Maslach, C., & Jackson, S. E. (1981). *Maslach burnout inventory – ES form (MBI)* [Database record]. APA PsycTests.

McLean, S., Wade, T. D., & Encel, J. S. (2003). The contribution of therapist beliefs to psychological distress in therapists: An investigation of vicarious traumatization, burnout and symptoms of avoidance and intrusion. *Behavioural and Cognitive Psychotherapy*, 31(4), 417–428.

McLeod, J. (2022). How students use deliberate practice during the first stage of counsellor training. *Counselling and Psychotherapy Research*, 22(1), 207–218.

McMahon, T. (1999). Is reflective practice synonymous with action research? *Educational Action Research*, 7(1), 163–169. https://doi.org/10.1080/09650799900200080

Mehr, K. E., Ladany, N., & Caskie, G. I. (2010). Trainee nondisclosure in supervision: What are they not telling you? *Counselling and Psychotherapy research*, 10(2), 103–113.

Meyer, J. M., Farrell, N. R., Kemp, J. J., Blakey, S. M., & Deacon, B. J. (2014). Why do clinicians exclude anxious clients from exposure therapy? *Behaviour Research and Therapy*, 54, 49–53. https://doi.org/10.1016/j.brat.2014.01.004

Meyer, J. M., Kelly, P. J., & Deacon, B. J. (2020). Therapist beliefs about exposure therapy implementation. *The Cognitive Behaviour Therapist*, 13, 13. https://doi.org/10.1017/S1754470X20000112

Miller, G. E. (1990). The assessment of clinical skills/competence/performance. *Academic Medicine*, 65, 63–67.

Milne, D. (2020). Preventing harm related to CBT supervision: A theoretical review and preliminary framework. *The Cognitive Behaviour Therapist*, 13, e54.

Milne, D., & Dunkerley, C. (2010). Towards evidence-based clinical supervision: The development and evaluation of four CBT guidelines. *The Cognitive Behaviour Therapist*, 3.

Milne, D. L., Leck, C., & Choudhri, N. Z. (2009). Collusion in clinical supervision: Literature review and case study in self reflection. *The Cognitive Behaviour Therapist*, 2.

Milne, D. L., & Reiser, R. P. (2014). A scale for rating competence in CBT supervision. In *The Wiley international handbook of clinical supervision* (p. 402). John Wiley & Sons, Ltd.

Milne, D. L., Reiser, R. P., Cliffe, T., & Raine, R. (2011). SAGE: Preliminary evaluation of an instrument for observing competence in CBT supervision. *The Cognitive Behaviour Therapist*, 4.

Milne, D. L., & Watkins, C. E. (2014). Defining and understanding clinical supervision: A functional approach. In Watkins Jr., C. E. & Milne, D. L. (Eds.). *The Wiley international handbook of clinical supervision*. John Wiley & Sons.

Moloney, P., & Kelly, P. (2004). Beck never lived in Birmingham: Why CBT may be a less useful treatment for psychological distress than is often supposed. *Clinical Psychology*, 4–10.

Moorey, S. (2013). *The interpersonal cycle worksheet*. Cognitive Connections. http://www.cognitiveconnections.co.uk

Moorey, S., & Lavender, A. (2019). *The therapeutic relationship in cognitive behavioural therapy*. Sage.

Murray, H., Grey, N., Warnock-Parkes, E., Kerr, A., Wild, J., Clark, D., & Ehlers, A. (2022). Ten misconceptions about trauma-focused CBT for PTSD. *The Cognitive Behaviour Therapist*, 15, e33. https://doi.org/10.1017/S1754470X22000307

Muse, K., Kennerley, H., & McManus, F. (2022). The why, what, when, who and how of assessing CBT competence to support lifelong learning. *The Cognitive Behaviour Therapist*, 15, e57.

Naeem, F., Phiri, P., Rathod, S., & Ayub, M. (2019). Cultural adaptation of cognitive–behavioural therapy. *British Journal of Psychiatric advances*, 25(6), 387–395.

National Collaborating Centre for Mental Health. (2019). *The improving access to psychological therapies manual*. NHS.

National Institute for Health and Clinical Excellence. (2005). Obsessive compulsive disorder and body dysmorphic disorder: Treatment. *Clinical Guidelines*, 31. https://www.nice.org.uk/guidance/cg31

National Institute for Health and Clinical Excellence. (2009). Depression: The treatment and management of depression in adults (update). *Clinical Guidance*. https://www.nice.org.uk/guidance/CG90

National Institute for Health and Clinical Excellence. (2011). Generalised anxiety disorder and panic disorder in adults: Management. *Clinical Guideline*, 113. https://www.nice.org.uk/guidance/cg113

National Institute for Health and Clinical Excellence. (2013). Social anxiety disorder: Recognition, assessment and treatment. *Clinical Guideline*, 159. https://www.nice.org.uk/guidance/cg159

National Institute for Health and Clinical Excellence. (2014). *Psychosis and schizophrenia in adults: Guideline on treatment and management (updated)*. https://nice.org.uk/guidance/CG178

National Institute for Health and Clinical Excellence. (2018). *Posttraumatic stress disorder*. NICE Guideline 116. https://www.nice.org.uk/guidance/ng116

Nelson, M. L., Barnes, K. L., Evans, A. L., & Triggiano, P. J. (2008). Working with conflict in clinical supervision: Wise supervisors' perspectives. *Journal of Counseling Psychology*, 55(2), 172.

Newman, C. F. (2013). Training cognitive behavioral therapy supervisors: Didactics, simulated practice, and 'metasupervision'. *Journal of Cognitive Psychotherapy*, 27, 5–18.

Ottingerová, L., Halamová, J., & Szitás, D. (2026). Experiential therapies including Chairwork: A systematic review of randomized controlled trials. *Frontiers in Psychology*, 16, 1692630.

Padesky, C. A. (1993). *Socratic questioning: Changing minds or guiding discovery?* Invited keynote address presented at the 1993 European Congress of Behaviour and Cognitive Therapies, London. https://www.padesky.com/clinicalcorner/publications

Padesky, C. A. (2005). *Supervision worksheet*. https://www.padesky.com/clinical-corner

Padesky, C. A., & Mooney, K. A. (1990). Clinical tip: Presenting the cognitive model to clients. *International Cognitive Therapy Newsletter*, 6(1), 13–14.

Painter, A. (2018). *Processing people!: The purpose and pitfalls of case management supervision provided for psychological wellbeing practitioners, working within Improving Access to Psychological Therapies (IAPT) services: A thematic analysis* (Doctoral dissertation, University of the West of England).

Palomo, M., Beinart, H., & Cooper, M. J. (2010). Development and validation of the Supervisory Relationship Questionnaire (SRQ) in UK trainee clinical psychologists. *British Journal of Clinical Psychology*, 49(2), 131–149.

Parker, Z. J., & Waller, G. (2017). Development and validation of the negative attitudes towards CBT Scale. *Behavioural and Cognitive Psychotherapy*, 45, 629–646.

Piaget, J. (1948). *The moral judgment of the child* (M. Gabain, trans.). Free Press.

Pieterse, A. L., Yang, E. J., Gordon, S., Wesley, K. M., Stevenson, L., & Mecca, K. A. (2025). Examining experiences of racism in clinical supervision: An exploratory study. *The Clinical Supervisor*, 1–23.

Pilling, S., & Roth, A. D. (2014). The competent clinical supervisor: The Wiley international handbook of clinical supervision. In Watkins Jr, C. E. & Milne, D. L. (Eds.) *The Wiley international handbook of clinical supervision* (pp. 20–37). John Wiley & Sons.

Presley, V. (2025). 'It's not you, it's me': Addressing therapist schemas during CBT training and beyond. In Roscoe, J. (Ed.) *Becoming a CBT therapist: Thriving in training and beyond* (pp. 140–151). Routledge.

Presley, V. L., Jones, G., & Marczak, M. (2023). The relationship between therapist experiential avoidance and observed CBT competence during training: A preliminary investigation. *The Cognitive Behaviour Therapist*, 16, e15.

Proctor, B. (1994). Supervision – competence, confidence, accountability. *British Journal of Guidance & Counselling*, 22, 309–318.

Pugh, M. (2019). A little less talk, a little more action: A dialogical approach to cognitive therapy. *The Cognitive Behaviour Therapist*, 12, e47.

Pugh, M., & Bell, T. (2020). Process-based chairwork: Applications and innovations in the time of COVID-19. *European Journal of Counselling Theory, Research, and Practice*, 4, 1–8.

Pugh, M., Bell, T., Waller, G., & Petrova, E. (2021). Attitudes and applications of chairwork amongst CBT therapists: A preliminary survey. *The Cognitive Behaviour Therapist*, 14, e21.

Pugh, M., & Margetts, A. (2020). Are you sitting (un) comfortably? Action-based supervision and supervisory drift. *The Cognitive Behaviour Therapist*, 13, e17.

Purdon, C., & Clark, D. A. (1993). Obsessive intrusive thoughts in nonclinical subjects. Part I. Content and relation with depressive, anxious and obsessional symptoms. *Behaviour Research and Therapy*, 31(8), 713–720.

Purnell, L., Chiu, K., Bhutani, G. E., Grey, N., El-Leithy, S., & Meiser-Stedman, R. (2024). Clinicians' perspectives on retraumatisation during trauma-focused interventions for post-traumatic stress disorder: A survey of UK mental health professionals. *Journal of Anxiety Disorders*, 106, 102913.

Rakovshik, S. G., McManus, F., Vazquez-Montes, M., Muse, K., & Ougrin, D. (2016). Is supervision necessary? Examining the effects of internet-based CBT training with and without supervision. *Journal of Consulting and Clinical Psychology*, 84(3), 191.

Reiser, R. P., Cliffe, T., & Milne, D. L. (2018). An improved competence rating scale for CBT supervision: Short-SAGE. *The Cognitive Behaviour Therapist*, 11, e7.

Rizq, R. (2012). The perversion of care: Psychological therapies in a time of IAPT. *Psychodynamic Practice*, 18(1), 7–24.

Robichaud, M., Koerner, N., & Dugas, M. J. (2019). *Cognitive behavioral treatment for generalized anxiety disorder: From science to practice*. Routledge.

Robinson, S., Kellett, S., King, I., & Keating, V. (2012). Role transition from mental health nurse to IAPT high intensity psychological therapist. *Behavioural and Cognitive Psychotherapy*, 40, 351–366. https://doi.org/10.1017/S1352465811000683

Rodwell, D., Kent, T., & Hale, L. (2023). Trainee clinical psychologists' views on the facilitators and barriers to cognitive behavioural practice: A thematic exploration. *Clinical Psychology Forum*, 362, 25).

Roscoe, J. (2020a). Sending out an SoS: The search for a clear definition of supervision of supervision. *CBT Today*, 48(4), 14–15.

Roscoe, J. (2020b). Rethinking therapist drift: Incompetence or ingenuity? *CBT Today*, 48(1), 10–11.

Roscoe, J. (2021a). Maximizing trainee cognitive behavioral therapists use of clinical supervision: Can a bespoke workshop help to broaden their horizons? *Journal of Applied Psychology and Social Science*, 6(1), 58–89.

Roscoe, J. (2021b). Conceptualising and managing supervisory drift. *The Cognitive Behaviour Therapist*, 14, E37. https://doi.org/10.1017/S1754470X21000350

Roscoe, J. (2021c). *Therapist schema and supervisory drift: A conceptual model*. BABCP Annual Conference, Belfast, Open Paper, 9 September.

Roscoe, J. (2021d). Your worth is not your recovery rate. *CBT Today*, 49(4), 7–9.

Roscoe, J. (2023a). Is role transition the 'elephant in the room' during CBT training? *CBT Today*, 51, 16–17.

Roscoe, J. (2023b). *Therapist schemas: What they are, why they matter and what we can do about them*. BABCP Annual Conference, Cardiff, Skills Class, July 2023.

Roscoe, J. (2026). *So. . .what is your supervision question then? – Helping supervisors and supervisees to keep supervision 'on track'*. BABCP Supervision Special Interest Group Conference, June 2026.

Roscoe, J., Bates, E. A., & Blackley, R. (2022b). 'It was like the unicorn of the therapeutic world': CBT trainee experiences of acquiring skills in guided discovery. *The Cognitive Behaviour Therapist*, 15, E32. https://doi.org/10.1017/S1754470X22000277

Roscoe, J., & Campbell-Lee, D. (2025). Keeping the shore in sight – how to be flexible in your practice whilst retaining the core principles of CBT. In Roscoe, J. (Ed.) *Becoming a CBT therapist: Thriving in training and beyond*. Routledge.

Roscoe, J., & Scullane, N. (2025). Supervising other CBT practitioners. In Roscoe, J. (Ed.) *Becoming a CBT therapist: Thriving in training and beyond*. Routledge.

Roscoe, J., & Taylor, J. (2023). Maladaptive therapist schemas in CBT practice, training and supervision: A scoping review. *Clinical Psychology & Psychotherapy*, 1–18. https://doi.org/10.1002/cpp.2802

Roscoe, J., Taylor, J., Harrington, R., & Wilbraham, S. (2022a). CBT supervision behind closed doors: Supervisor and supervisee reflections on their expectations and use of clinical supervision. *Counselling and Psychotherapy Research*, 22(4), 1056–1067. https://doi.org/10.1002/capr.12572

Roscoe, J., & Wilbraham, S. (2024). 'When it goes well, it works fantastically': Motivations to train and their impact on the practice of CBT. *The Cognitive Behaviour Therapist*, 17, e6.

Roth, A. D., & Pilling, S. (2007). *The competences required to deliver effective cognititve and behavioural therapy for people with depression and with anxiety disorders*. Department of Health.

Roth, A. D., & Pilling, S. (2008). *A competence framework for the supervision of psychological therapies*. https://www.ucl.ac.uk/pals/sites/pals/files/background_document_supervision_competences_july_2015.pdf

Roth, A. D., Pilling, S., & Turner, J. (2010). Therapist training and supervision in clinical trials: Implications for clinical practice. *Behavioural and Cognitive Psychotherapy*, 38, 291–302.

Rye, M., Rognmo, K., Aarons, G. A., & Skre, I. (2019). Attitudes towards the use of routine outcome monitoring of psychological therapies among mental health providers: The EBPAS–ROM. *Administration and Policy in Mental Health and Mental Health Services Research*, 46(6), 833–846.

Sacks, D., & Vaz, A. (2023). The use of deliberate practice in cognitive behavioral therapy supervision: From declarative to procedural knowledge. In Terjesen, M. D. & Del Vecchio, T. (Eds.) *Handbook of training and supervision in cognitive behavioral therapy* (pp. 259–272). Cham: Springer International Publishing.

Salkovskis, P. M., Sighvatsson, M. B., & Sigurdsson, J. F. (2023). How effective psychological treatments work: Mechanisms of change in cognitive behavioural therapy and beyond. *Behavioural and Cognitive Psychotherapy*, 51(6), 595–615.

Samstag, L. W., Muran, J. C., & Safran, J. D. (2003). Defining and identifying alliance ruptures. In Charman, D. P. (Ed.) *Core processes in brief psychodynamic psychotherapy* (pp. 203–230). Routledge.

Schulte, D., & Eifert, G. H. (2002). What to do when manuals fail? The dual model of psychotherapy. *Clinical Psychology: Science and Practice*, 9(3), 312.

Scott, M. J. (2020). Ensuring that the Improving Access to Psychological Therapies (IAPT) programme does what it says on the tin. *The British Journal of Clinical Psychology*, 60(1), 38.

Segal, Z. V. (1988). Appraisal of the self-schema construct in cognitive models of depression. *Psychological Bulletin*, 103(2), 147–162. https://doi.org/10.1037/0033-2909.103.2.147

Shaw, B. F., Elkin, I., Yamaguchi, J., Olmsted, M., Vallis, T. M., Dobson, K. S., Lowery, A, Sotsky, S. M., Watkins, J. T., & Imber, S. D. (1999). Therapist competence ratings in relation to clinical outcome in cognitive therapy of depression. *Journal of Consulting and Clinical Psychology*, 67(6), 837.

Simpson-Southward, C., Waller, G., & Hardy, G. (2018). Supervisor practice when guiding therapists working with depression: The impact of supervisor and patient characteristics. *The Cognitive Behaviour Therapist*, 11, E9. https://doi.org/10.1017/S1754470X18000089

Skovholt, T. M., & Jennings, L. (Eds.). (2017). *Master therapists: Exploring expertise in therapy and counseling*. Oxford University Press.

Spännargård, Å., Fagernäs, S., & Alfonsson, S. (2025). Discrepancies between guidelines, preferences and actual activities in psychotherapy supervision. *Counselling and Psychotherapy Research*, 25(1), e12824.

Speers, A. J., Bhullar, N., Cosh, S., & Wootton, B. M. (2022). Correlates of therapist drift in psychological practice: A systematic review of therapist characteristics. *Clinical Psychology Review*, 93, 102132. https://doi.org/10.1016/j.cpr.2022.102132

Spitzer, R. L., Kroenke, K., & Williams, J. B. W. (1999). Validation and utility of a self-report version of the PRIME-MD: The PHQ primary care study. *Journal of the American Medical Association*, 202(18), 1737–1744. https://doi.org/10.1001/jama.282.18.1737

Stoltenberg, C. (1981). Approaching supervision from a developmental perspective: The counselor complexity model. *Journal of counseling Psychology*, 28(1), 59.

Stoltenberg, C. D., & McNeill, B. (2010). *IDM supervision: An integrative developmental model for supervising counsellors and therapists*. Routledge.

Sue, D. W., Alsaidi, S., Awad, M. N., Glaeser, E., Calle, C. Z., & Mendez, N. (2019). Disarming racial microaggressions: Microintervention strategies for targets, White allies, and bystanders. *American Psychologist*, 74(1), 128.74(1), 128.

Swift, J. K., Callahan, J. L., Rousmaniere, T. G., Whipple, J. L., Dexter, K., & Wrape, E. R. (2015). Using client outcome monitoring as a tool for supervision. *Psychotherapy*, 52(2), 180.

Taylor, J. R., & Sims, M. (2025). To understand the experiences of autistic counsellors: A United Kingdom phenomenological study. *Counselling and Psychotherapy Research*, 25(2), e12839.

Taylor, K. N., Gordon, K., Grist, S., & Olding, C. (2012). Developing supervisory competence: Preliminary data on the impact of CBT supervision training. *The Cognitive Behaviour Therapist*, 5(4), 83–92.

Thorndike, E. L. (1920). A constant error in psychological ratings. *Journal of Applied Psychology*, 4, 25–29.

Townend, M., Iannetta, L., & Freeston, M. H. (2002). Clinical supervision in practice: A survey of UK cognitive behavioural psychotherapists accredited by the BABCP. *Behavioural and Cognitive Psychotherapy*, 30, 485.

Vaz, A., McLeod, J., & Nissen-Lie, H. A. (2025). Rethinking psychotherapy training and supervision: The case for deliberate practice. *Journal of Clinical Psychology*, 81(6), 393–398.

Vekaria, B., Thomas, T., Phiri, P., & Ononaiye, M. (2023). Exploring the supervisory relationship in the context of culturally responsive supervision: A supervisee's perspective. *The Cognitive Behaviour Therapist*, 16, E22. https://doi.org/10.1017/S1754470X23000168

Vygotsky, L. S. (1978). *Mind in society: The development of higher psychological processes*. Harvard University Press.

Wade, T. D., & Waller, G. (2025). Ten generic competences to improve outcomes of cognitive behaviour therapy: Evidence, postulated processes, and clinical implications. *Behaviour Research and Therapy*, 104826.

Wainwright, N. A. (2010). *The development of the Leeds Alliance in Supervision Scale (LASS): A brief sessional measure of the supervisory alliance*. https://etheses.whiterose.ac.uk/1118/

Waller, G. (2009). Evidence-based treatment and therapist drift. *Behaviour Research and Therapy*, 47, 119–127. https://doi.org/10.1016/j.brat.2008.10.018

Waltman, S., Hall, B. C., McFarr, L. M., Beck, A. T., & Creed, T. A. (2017). In-session stuck points and pitfalls of community clinicians learning CBT: Qualitative investigation. *Cognitive and Behavioral Practice*, 24, 256–267.

Weck, F., Jakob, M., Neng, J. M., Höfling, V., Grikscheit, F., & Bohus, M. (2016). The effects of bug-in-the-eye supervision on therapeutic alliance and therapist competence in cognitive-behavioural therapy: A randomized controlled trial. *Clinical Psychology & Psychotherapy*, 23(5), 386–396.

Wedge, P. (2005). *The development of the homework adherence and competence scale (HAACS): A measure for assessing therapist adherence and competence in administering homework assignments within cognitive behaviour therapy: A thesis presented in partial fulfilment of the requirements for the degree of Master of Arts in Psychology at Massey University* (Doctoral dissertation, Massey University).

Weissman, A. N., & Beck, A. T. (1978). Development and validation of the dysfunctional attitude scale: A preliminary investigation. Paper presented at the Annual Meeting of The American Educational Research Association, Toronto, Ontario.

Wilcockson, M. (2022). Conflicts of identity – how counsellors practice CBT 5 years post qualification. *Sciences*, 11, 42–50. https://doi.org/10.11648/j.pbs.20221102.11

Wilcockson, M. D. (2020). Transition to cognitive behavioural therapy from different core professional backgrounds: Three grounded theory studies. *The Cognitive Behaviour Therapist*, 13, E35. https://doi.org/10.1017/S1754470X20000331

Williams, M. T., Faber, S. C., & Duniya, C. (2022). Being an anti-racist clinician. *The Cognitive Behaviour Therapist*, 15, e19.

Wolff, S., & Auckenthaler, A. (2014). Processes of theoretical orientation development in CBT trainees: What internal processes do psychotherapists in training undergo as they 'integrate'? *Journal of Psychotherapy Integration*, 24, 223–237.

Worthless, I. M., Competent, U. R., & Lemonde-Terrible, O. (2002). And finally . . . . . . cognitive therapy training stress disorder: A cognitive perspective. *Behavioural and Cognitive Psychotherapy*, 30, 365–374.

Young, J. E., & Beck, A. T. (1980). *Cognitive therapy scale*. Unpublished manuscript. University of Pennsylvania.

Yourman, D. B. (2003). Trainee disclosure in psychotherapy supervision: The impact of shame. *Journal of Clinical Psychology*, 59(5), 601–609.

Index

For Product Safety Concerns and Information please contact our EU representative GPSR@taylorandfrancis.com
Taylor & Francis Verlag GmbH, Kaufingerstraße 24, 80331 München, Germany

www.ingramcontent.com/pod-product-compliance
Ingram Content Group UK Ltd.
Pitfield, Milton Keynes, MK11 3LW, UK
UKHW022020180926
475701UK00005B/936

* 9 7 8 1 0 3 2 9 6 7 6 1 5 *